How to Finish This Book (And Just About Anything Else):
Proven Methods for Productivity, Taking Action, and Execution

By Peter Hollins

Author and Researcher at petehollins.com

Table of Contents

INTRODUCTION 5

CHAPTER 1: GET RID OF MENTAL CLUTTER WITH BRAIN DUMPING 11

CHAPTER 2: SEPARATE TASKS BASED ON IMPORTANCE WITH THE 1-3-5 RULE 23

CHAPTER 3: WORK WITH THE TIME BLOCKING METHOD 33

CHAPTER 4: FIND THE WHY BEHIND YOUR TASKS 45

CHAPTER 5: SAY NO TO OVERLOADED TO-DO LISTS WITH 3 + 2 RULE 53

CHAPTER 6: SLUMP MODE PROTOCOL 63

CHAPTER 7: CONSOLIDATE REPETITIVE TASKS USING THE DRY PRINCIPLE 77

CHAPTER 8: AVOID ZERO DAYS 85

CHAPTER 9: USE A SINGLE SOURCE OF TRUTH 97

CHAPTER 10: MAXIMIZE YOUR DOWNTIME WITH TIME POCKETS 107

CHAPTER 11: DESTROY TIME CRATERS 117

CHAPTER 12: SAY NO WITH THE HOURGLASS METHOD 129

CHAPTER 13: N.E.T 141

CHAPTER 14: MONK MODE 151

CHAPTER 15: TOUCH IT ONCE PRINCIPLE 159

CHAPTER 16: SELF-COMPETITION 169

CHAPTER 17: PRODUCTIVE COGNITIVE LOAD 181

CHAPTER 18: WORK BACKWARDS 195

CHAPTER 19: CLEAN SLATE METHOD 205

CHAPTER 20: FOCUS FUNNEL 215

CONCLUSION 229

Introduction

"Time is the most valuable coin in your life. You and you alone will determine how that coin will be spent. Be careful that you do not let other people spend it for you."

- **Carl Sandburg**

Before we charge ahead with our book on productivity, let's not assume that we already know what productivity *is*.

Let's consider a few possible definitions:

Productivity: A measure of economic performance

Productivity: The output of goods and services relative to the input required to generate them

Productivity: The rate (i.e. speed) at which a person, a company, or an entire country does useful work

You can already see that these definitions raise a few questions:

Is productivity just about money?

Does speed actually matter? Relative to what?

And what counts as "useful" work, anyway?

In this book, we're going to be working from an expanded view of productivity. It's not about merely increasing "output" or blindly going faster. It's not about money. Rather, it's a question of simplicity, meaning, focus, and quality over quantity.

Conventional productivity advice is often just "hustle culture" in disguise.

If working three hours is good, then working four must be better, and five better still, right?

Maybe not. If you've picked up this book, it's likely that you already know that this formula (productivity = do more*)* doesn't always work out in real life.

Our expanded definition:

Productivity: The degree to which you make intentional, elegant use of time towards a narrow set of consciously chosen and meaningful goals.

Richie Norton once said that "Productivity is to create asymmetrical situations where your one good input creates many good outputs."

Sounds great! But who defines "good outputs"?

We do!

Productivity is not just about how much you do, but how well you do it. It's about what your actions *mean*.

Becoming a more productive person doesn't mean working yourself to death, cutting corners, or treating your body and mind like a sweat shop.

It means adopting a mindset that allows you to take full ownership of the way you use time, so that you can start channeling it towards those things that matter most to you.

Signs You Are NOT Living Productively

- Do you struggle with procrastination, lack of motivation, boredom, and dread around work?
- Do you feel like the busiest day of your week is always tomorrow?
- Do you feel like your attention is constantly drained away by endless distractions, and your energy by endless chores?
- Do you feel like your life's mantra is, "I don't have the time"?
- Do you feel totally burnt out and overworked, but also like you haven't moved forward an inch?

If any of this resonates, then relax—you're in the right place. You *can* become a more productive person, and you can do it without beating yourself up or sacrificing what's important.

In the chapters that follow, we'll be exploring:

- How to cut through mental clutter and start focusing on what matters—and how to determine what really doesn't
- How to take control of time instead of letting it control you

- A magic word that will instantly make you more productive (spoiler: That word is *no*)
- How to stay on track day after day—even when you slip up or feel lazy
- How to build the life you want with the time you already have
- How to tune out distractions, insecurity, confusion, fear, and doubt
- How to work *with* your brain and body, rather than fight *against* them, so you naturally get the best out of yourself—without force or depletion

We're not talking about cheat codes and shortcuts that allow us to avoid effort. Instead, we're talking about **the art of right effort**—using your time, energy, and attention in the very best way you can.

How to Use This Book

The best way to use this book is to actually *use* it, not just read it!

Reading is passive.

Intellectually grasping a new idea doesn't automatically mean that your life changes.

And the fact that an idea is easy to understand doesn't mean it will be easy to implement.

Let's put it this way: Reading about productivity won't make you more productive in the same way that reading recipes won't cause food to magically appear!

The goal here is active application. Until they are actively applied, even the most sophisticated tools and techniques mean nothing.

We'll be exploring many different approaches, methods, and mindsets around productivity, how to be more disciplined, and how to consistently cultivate deeper clarity and focus... but the secret ingredient is your applied effort.

Some of these methods will speak to you, others less so. But if you consistently experiment, observe your results, and adjust as you go, you'll gain valuable insight.

You don't have to be perfect to get something from this book. You just have to be willing to make that jump between *knowing* and *doing*. And honestly? It's a very small jump!

Let's get started.

Chapter 1: Get Rid of Mental Clutter With Brain Dumping

"Who am I in the midst of this thought traffic?"

- **Rumi**

Have you ever had one of those days where it feels like you're getting *nothing* done, yet somehow, you've been rushing around for hours?

"I'm too busy to get anything done!"

Quite the paradox.

You have so much to do that you can't get anything done. Hmm.

The way many of us have organized our lives today is, frankly, a little insane.

- We start tasks but don't finish them.
- We think about something we want to do but then forget why it ever mattered in the first place.
- We have a dozen "open tabs" on our mental browsers, each of them stressing us out, and none of them ever resolving or progressing.
- We hold a thousand and one things in our minds and think at the speed of light… and still feel like we need to do even more!

When life feels like this, the concept of "productivity" hits in all the wrong ways.

How could you be better at time management when you don't feel like you have any time? How could you speed up when you can barely *keep up*? And how can you summon up more motivation and energy when you're exhausted and barely holding on as it is?

One of the biggest misconceptions about improving productivity and efficiency is that it's **additive**, i.e., you need to do *more*, you need to *increase*, or you need to *speed up*.

In this book, our approach is *not* to see our minds and live our lives like mere machines. Productivity is not about finding that special output dial and turning it up a few notches so that your life generates more value.

Instead, **productivity is about elegance**.

It's about creating a life that is neat, clean, and logically sound.

- What productivity isn't: Forcefully cranking up the output dial no matter the cost
- What productivity is: Fine-tuning and adjusting that dial to discover the optimal balance between input and output

I'm pretty sure you feel "busy." But is this busyness a result of deep and targeted work on meaningful tasks that you've intentionally chosen?

Or… are you really just straining under a state of constant mental buffering, distraction, fragmentation, and overload?

Our brains will not work as well when they're wasting time and energy navigating unnecessary mental clutter. This includes:

- Nagging deadlines
- Boring errands
- Little chores and tasks that hang over you
- Things you've forgotten, then remembered, then forgotten again
- Vague concerns and unresolved issues
- "Life admin"
- Random thoughts and worries
- Emails, messages, notifications…

The more of this stuff you try to hold in your head at once, the more you slow yourself down. Your perception of being cognitively "full" and emotionally overwhelmed increases, but your actual output and productivity stays the same… or, let's be honest, decreases.

It may seem a little counterintuitive at first to imagine that **you can do less and be more productive**.

But you can. And you *should*.

Brain dumping is a way to clear the decks, tidy up your mental workspace, and get rid of the energy-sucking brain clutter that is slowing you down.

The big idea is to close every loop that you open. Tie up every thread. Your goal is not to wade through mental clutter or add to it, but to reduce your cognitive load so that:

- You have more energy available for what matters
- You're more focused
- Your work is deeper and more meaningful

As an extra bonus, your stress and anxiety levels are likely to drop, and you'll be in that golden "**act, don't react**" zone. You'll stop overthinking, and you'll stop dwelling in that disempowered, putting-out-fires-mode.

When you're wading through brain junk, you're on the back foot and spending a lot of your life force just trying to stay in the same place. But when you streamline and cut out the fluff, you're better able to solve problems, create, prioritize, and follow through on what actually matters to you.

Brain dumping: Taking all the mental junk and clutter out of your head, and putting it onto paper instead (here, digital tools and apps count).

To get on top of house clutter and disorder, you don't need to buy more stuff or throw everything out in frustration, right? You simply need better organization, storage, and flow.

It's the same with cognitive clutter. You don't need more things to think about, nor do you need to get burnt out and give up on everything because you're overwhelmed. You simply need better mental organization, storage, and flow.

That's what brain dumping is all about. Here are some ways to start integrating brain dumping into your daily routine.

Start Your Day With a 10-Minute Unload (Then Highlight 3 Priorities)

You might sit down to do your scheduled tasks for the day but discover that you're not really *there*. Your head's all over the place and you're scattered.

Maybe it's like some vague, unfinished task is hovering just on the edge of your awareness, or maybe there are a thousand little distractions and disruptions incessantly popping into your mind.

"What about that email you haven't sent? What about this evening? What about that thing you were supposed to buy? What about...?"

You're not lazy, and you're not procrastinating. But you *are* trying to do something pretty difficult: wade through a cluttered and crowded mental house!

Here, "productivity" doesn't mean white-knuckling it through the chaotic feelings and forcing yourself to grind through. It means deliberately pausing to clear your mind and remove what's getting in the way.

- Set a timer for ten minutes.
- Put everything that's swimming around in your head down onto paper, or type it out.
- Include every single thought, concern, question, idea, or outstanding task. Don't worry about being structured, and don't worry about solving or organizing anything. Just imagine you are mentally dumping things into a big box called "brain stuff."
- When the timer goes off, stop.
- Take a deep breath. Consciously tell yourself that you don't have to hold all this in your mind anymore. Let the written words do your remembering so you don't have to.
- The final step is to quickly go through the "brain stuff" box and pick out three things that matter the most to you today. **Just three things, just today.**

Everything else in the box can be delegated or scheduled for consideration at some other time.

Realistically? A lot of what you put in this box will be genuine trash that you can safely ignore.

Once you've cleared your mind and identified your priorities in this way, you can usually get to work on your task with more focus and ease.

If little thoughts *do* rear their head, tell yourself politely: "Thank you, Brain, you've already brought that to my attention, and I've already noted it down. I will get to everything at the right time and in the right order. *Right now*, I'm focusing on my priorities."

Sort Your Dump With a Simple 3-Box framework

If your thought clutter is of the *illogical rumination* type, then simply writing things down may be enough. It's like swatting away flies. Putting things down in black and white can instantly make them seem more manageable, more defined, and less intimidating.

However, like with most clutter, there are sometimes useful things mixed in with the junk. Once you've taken ten minutes to get everything out of your brain box and down onto paper, take a moment to sort through it all.

A big part of your stress and disorganization comes from:

- The sheer volume of clutter ("it's all too much!")

- The chaos and mixed-up-ness of the clutter ("I can't tell what's important and what isn't!")

Now, you've put things down in words, and you've pulled out the three **most important** and **most urgent** things. These are your Do Today tasks. These are the loops you're working on closing right now. Identifying them will keep you focused, on-task, and *calm*.

Now, there are two more boxes we can sort our brain clutter into:

- **Schedule or Delegate**
    - These are things that are *important, but not urgent.*
    - They need to be done, but not right now. You need to set a time when you'll do them, or when someone else might do them.
- **Save for Later**
    - These things are *not urgent, and may or may not be important.*
    - You may not be able to take any action on them right now, but you can schedule a time/reminder in the future when you'll revisit these ideas.

It doesn't take long to sort out your random thoughts into these three boxes. Once you start this practice, in fact, you may notice how few open threads and loops it really takes to have you feeling completely overwhelmed!

On the other hand, you may be surprised by how quickly a little organization brings more clarity and focus.

Often, stressed, overwhelmed, and "busy" people don't objectively have more on their plates than organized, focused, and efficient people. The latter are just more prepared.

"I'm too busy to get anything done!" really means "I'm wasting time and energy on things that don't matter."

Spend your mental energy on only a handful of things at once, and strategically set aside the rest.

Use a "Night Dump" to Sleep More Peacefully and Start Tomorrow Prepared

If your brain is cluttered, your sleep will soon start feeling like worrying with your eyes closed.

If your brain has been racing and churning all day, why should it suddenly stop just because it's midnight and you're exhausted?

Being cognitively cluttered—i.e., overthinking—actually interferes with two important processes:

- Your active and effortful work
- Your rest and recuperation

If you spend your daylight waking hours in an inefficient fluster, *and* your rest time feeling wired up and unable to switch off, then you're doing a worst-of-both-worlds maneuver that will burn you out fast.

The charmingly named "night dump" will bring some relief, allowing you to work when you're working, and rest when you're resting.

- Just before you go to sleep, take five minutes to write down whatever's been weighing on you that day. This means unfinished business, nagging worries, little resentments or fears, residual bits of annoyance or everyday stress.
- This is not journaling—just a few bullet points or notes will be enough to tell your brain that things are in hand, and that it does *not* need to keep reminding you of them all night.
- When you're done, pause to deliberately acknowledge that these things are tomorrow's things. You may like to add a little creative visualization. For example, when you close the journal cover, imagine that the words themselves are going to sleep, and will be quiet until morning.
- One optional step: Decide early which the three things you'd like to focus on tomorrow. This will make you less anxious and

distractable, and help you wake up feeling purposeful.

Brain dumping is one of those easy, obvious habits that nevertheless has the power to dramatically change your life. Remember, you don't have to solve everything completely or do everything at once. Just untangle the first few knots and get to work on those. The rest is work for another day.

Long story short: Stop giving your brain more than it can handle.

It was built for thinking—not for storing every single bit of random data that comes your way.

Process things, then let them go. Keep notes and travel light!

Chapter 2: Separate Tasks Based on Importance with the 1-3-5 Rule

"I must create a system, or be enslaved by another man's. I will not reason and compare: my business is to create."

- **William Blake**

One unspoken Law of Productivity that we will return to again and again throughout this book: **Not all tasks are created equal.**

With that in mind, it is inherently true that we cannot approach every task in exactly the same way.

When you're anxious, overthinking, overwhelmed, or expecting too much of yourself, you're making an error: "*All* of these tasks are equally important."

But are they?

You may unwittingly send yourself this message every time you create a To Do list. Think about it: No matter what the item is, its position on the list already implies that it shares equal status with all the other items, and carries the same weight.

But does it?

"Having priorities" goes a lot deeper than just identifying what looks to be the most important task at any one time.

Ranking things in terms of importance is one thing, but truly understanding our priorities requires that we make a pretty serious mindset shift: *We are not here just to complete tasks.* The tasks we do flow from the goals that we ourselves have freely chosen.

That's a subtle but very important distinction.

We need to proactively create a system to filter out what matters most to us—and that's a question of values, purpose, and meaning.

Without our own system, we get swallowed into other people's, or else we just ride along with whatever momentum existed before us. We are reactive, not proactive. This means:

- We waste our time on low-impact work
- We waste our energy managing stress that never needed to exist in the first place
- We waste our focus pursuing things we don't care about

The 1-3-5 Rule is a way to be proactive, deliberate, and focused about how your time and energy are used, and it's easy to follow. All you do is plan each and every day around **1 big task, 3 medium tasks, and 5 small tasks.**

This balance more closely resembles the way our brains naturally want to work. We are not machines, and we do not work linearly. Every task tends to contain:

- A single most important component that deserves our full concentration.
    - Completing it leads to a big dopamine boost and sense of reward.
- A few that require our attention but not total devotion.
    - A moderate balance between effort and reward.
- And the rest are small, everyday wins that are really just there to keep the engines running.
    - Low-hanging fruit and easy wins that boost motivation to keep going.

We struggle not because of the tasks themselves, but because we have given too much to a task that didn't deserve it.

Not everything warrants our time and attention, and when it does, it doesn't necessarily require *all* of it.

Clearly teasing these things apart prevents overwhelm, brings clarity, and taps into the brain's reward system by balancing challenge with achievability.

Identify Your One Big Task

To reiterate, not all tasks are created equal.

Who decides how to rank them?

It should be *you*!

If you fail to identify for yourself what this single important and non-negotiable task is, you risk allowing lazy habit, momentum, or other people to take over and decide for you.

- Just because other people tell you something is urgent doesn't automatically mean it is.
- Just because a peer has decided that a certain task holds the most value for them doesn't mean that it has to hold the most value for you.
- Just because you find a task enjoyable doesn't necessarily mean that it drives meaningful progress.

First, brainstorm all the tasks you need to do.

Take a few moments to list everything out—no matter how enormous or how trivial it may seem. This exercise alone may be illuminating; have you only been making assumptions and guesses about what needs to be done?

Next, pick out the most important thing.

Your One Big Task should do most of the heavy lifting. That means it needs to create the highest amount of value, instigate the greatest degree of movement, or otherwise bring the highest yield to the table.

Here are some other things it has to be:

- Genuinely **meaningful** – not just urgent.

- **Specific** – it needs to speak to a precise goal and intention.
- Most **impactful** – there may be plenty of helpful little things you could do, but your One Big Task is impactful enough that it's definitive, i.e., it could stand alone.

Your One Big Task could be anything. It depends on your goals, resources, and constraints.

It could be writing an important email, creating a plan or key outline, having a difficult conversation, booking an important flight, making a key decision, completing a research paper, or hiring a new team member.

Tip: Your One Big thing deserves you at your best, so schedule work on this task for those times of day when you're feeling alert, energized, and focused.

Bonus tip: If your One Big Thing is a little too big, that's OK. Break it down and tackle it in stages.

Plan Your Three Medium Tasks

The beauty of this method is in how it encourages you to keep things simple and straightforward. It's a time management tool as well as a method for self-regulation—seeing just a few key tasks on your To Do list every day is psychologically easier and more rewarding.

"Medium" tasks do matter, but they don't require the absolute best of us. The approach here is *balance*.

You want to give these tasks their due without letting them expand, creep, or take over too much.

That means it's important to **set upper and lower bounds for the attention and focus you are willing to invest.** To put this another way: These things need to be done, but they don't need to be done first, nor do they need to be done perfectly.

They're necessary supportive tasks, such as:

- Attending meetings or lectures
- Reading additional papers and reports
- Preparing for a conversation
- Weighing up options
- Research

Now that you know what your One Big Task is, consider the rest of what's on your plate and ask what *three things* are most able to support you in achieving it.

Tip: The way to keep these important-but-not-that-important tasks from eating up more attention than they need to is to set firm time limits. Schedule a block of say 45 or 60 minutes, then reassess once your alarm goes off. If you don't set time limits, you risk getting distracted away from the task that matters more.

If you like, batch similar tasks together to stay in the same mental gear and cut down on context-switching.

Bonus tip: Be realistic. When you're starting out, it's usually better to under-commit than to expect too much and then disappoint yourself. Aim small; you'll give yourself the reward of over-delivering.

Select Five Small Tasks

Your small tasks are also supportive, but they're... well, small. These are the things that will take you ten minutes or less to do:

- Reorganizing some files
- Sending a quick message
- RSVPing to an invitation
- Throwing something away
- Making a quick reservation
- Double-checking some details

Many of these tasks may seem too small to even bother with. Should we really be putting them on our To Do list at all?

Yes! There are a few good reasons for doing so:

Reason 1: You clear mental clutter, and that not only feels great, it also brings focus and clarity.

Reason 2: You build motivation. Every completed task is a little rewarding dopamine boost, which then inspires you to keep going.

Reason 3: You build momentum. These tasks may be small, but they get you *moving*. And once you're moving, you can turn your attention to bigger things.

By identifying these small tasks ahead of time, you already know that it's not the end of the world if you don't complete all of them. These things are complementary and extra bonuses—they are not meant to dominate your thoughts or leave you feeling guilty or obligated.

If you don't get around to a small task, let it go without guilt. Schedule it for tomorrow, or just drop it if possible.

OK, so now you have three different categories, but you still don't have a *system* that helps you manage yourself day to day. Here are some additional tips on how to proceed once you've identified what's important, and what isn't.

- **Be flexible.** The system serves you; you don't serve the system. Life is unpredictable. If something doesn't come together every now and again, just make modifications and move on.
- **Adjust as you go.** The 1-3-5 system is something to help you manage your tasks, it's not meant to be another task. Feel free to adjust the number of tasks you can manage according to your preferences, goals, and

limits. For example, you might prefer a 1-2-3 ratio.
- **Spend yourself wisely.** As a rule, spend your peak energy and focus (typically in the morning) on the big task, and gradually move to medium and small tasks as the day wears on. Don't attempt the big task when you're depleted or overwhelmed, and don't waste peak energy on small errands.
- **Have a routine.** Take a few minutes each morning or evening to create and review your 1-3-5 list. Make time to celebrate wins—no matter how small. If you've fallen short, pay attention to what went well and commit to doing more the following day. Don't beat yourself up; consistency always matters more than perfection.
- **Monitor your progress.** Every week or month, ask yourself:
    - What are the tasks I'm routinely leaving undone? Why?
    - What is the time of day I'm most productive?
    - Am I consistently achieving what I set out to?
    - Is my appraisal of the importance of different tasks accurate?

It's completely normal to need to fine-tune, reassess, or go back to the drawing board now and then.

Your priorities will change; change with them.

What matters is that you are no longer sitting passively, waiting for tasks to come at you so you can deal with them whack-a-mole style. Instead, you are carving out a deliberate, strategic path through your day.

Chapter 3: Work With the Time Blocking Method

"You will never find time for anything. If you want time you must make it."

- **Charles Buxton**

How can you tell when your tasks are controlling you, rather than you controlling your tasks?

The signs are clear. Your day feels:

- Chaotic
- Scattered
- Reactive
- Stressful
- Wasteful
- Unproductive

To Do lists are certainly a handy tool and have their place, but the truth is that writing down a list of tasks doesn't tell you *when* to do a task, *how* to do it, or for *how long*.

A To Do list can't tell you what *not* to do.

It doesn't give you any clues about how the tasks fit with one another, or their relative importance.

Tasks are theoretically infinite.

What isn't? Time.

Instead of giving ourselves a daily set of things to accomplish, we can focus our intention on time, and how to budget it properly. When you block out portions of time, you not only create a visual expression of your priorities and your intentions, but you also create a **script**—a path to follow through the day.

Unlike a To Do list, time blocking gives you structure, definition, and direction. It lets you know very clearly whether you are on task, or not. No room for argument. This way, you cut down on decision fatigue, and you reduce opportunities for procrastination, distraction, and excuse-making.

The world is positively bursting at the seams with things that demand your energy, time, attention, and resources. Unless you consciously allocate your time in a way that suits your values and goals, then soon you won't have much left to call *your* time at all.

Time blocking: Allocating specific tasks to specific blocks of time throughout the day.

Popularized by Cal Newport, this method is simple yet powerful.

When you give every hour of your time a purpose, you start to treat time like the precious resource it is. Being time conscious means:

- **Understanding that time can be *invested*, or it can be *wasted*.** No matter what you choose to do, every hour of time *will* pass.

You get decide how much return you get on it, though.

- **There is not, nor will there ever be, "enough time."** The need to prioritize is simply a fact of life. There isn't time for everything, so ensure that the time you do have is spent on what matters most.
- **If you manage it well, there is always enough time to do what counts.** If you don't manage it well, you will never have enough of it.

Time can be a wonderful clarifier; if we make a commitment to do something at 9 a.m., then that's it—we either do it or we don't, and we have to face that fact. If our alarm goes off after an hour, then that's it—an hour really has passed and we cannot delude ourselves about what might, should, or could have been.

Have you ever suddenly found yourself at 6 p.m. wondering, "Where did the day go?"

The (mildly terrifying) answer to this is: It's gone. *You let it go.*

If we fail to structure our time, it dribbles away from us and we find ourselves at the mercy of distraction, disorganization, laziness, forgetfulness, and apathy.

Instead, here are some ways to use time blocking to reclaim that time and start making it work for you.

Block Your Recurring Activities First

When it comes to time blocking, you're essentially working backwards: you start by blocking off the periods in every day that will be committed to things like sleep, meals, workouts, or routine family obligations.

These are fixed commitments, and you need to agree with yourself that these are standing appointments that are simply never encroached upon.

This might explain why ultra-productive people are often obsessed with morning and evening routines. Once they have established a workable and productive framework around the flow of their day:

- They refuse to allow any creep or drift.
- They do not overbook themselves.
- They don't see their bedtimes or wake up times as negotiable.

These blocks are untouchable and the time they take is spoken for.

The eight or so hours of sleep you have every night is the biggest recurring activity, but here are some more examples:

A morning routine

You might block 7:00–8:00 a.m. for your full morning routine, including grooming, dressing, breakfast, journaling, enjoying a coffee, making your bed, or planning the day.

A repeat activity

You might block out every Wednesday evening from 6:00-7:30 p.m. for weekly rehearsal or brand practice.

Meal habits

You might block out a half hour for lunch at noon, and an hour and a half for the evening meal at 6:30 PM.

Other things you might consider recurring non-negotiables:

- Church
- Birthdays, anniversaries, and special holidays like Christmas
- Vacations and holidays, weekend activities
- Weekly or daily meetings
- Your evening routine
- The weekly shopping, planning, and meal prep
- Childcare
- Walking the dog

This step may seem pretty straightforward, but be honest with yourself—how often have you disregarded your own self-care, thrown away special family time, or neglected things like exercise or house maintenance so you could sacrifice that time to something else?

Being realistic about the time you actually have at your disposal prevents overcommitment, burnt out, unrealistic expectations, and boundary confusion.

Theme Your Day to Reduce Switching

It's your choice whether you'd like to split your calendar into *personal* and *professional* obligations, but the truth is, you only have one life, not two. Putting everything on one calendar forces you to acknowledge that, where time is concerned, we are all playing a zero-sum game.

Once your base schedule is done, you can start to think about the rest.

At a glance, you should be able to see how much "disposable time" you have on your hands to do all your other tasks, whether that's creative, administrative, collaborative, or strategic.

You might be tempted to launch in and start dividing the remaining time up into hour chunks. While there's nothing logically wrong with this, having many broken-up units of time across a single day has some serious disadvantages.

Imagine that every hour block has a narrow margin around it, the beginning and end:

- **The first 5-10 minutes:** You're warming up, settling in, getting yourself physically organized and comfortable, allowing your brain to switch into the right gear, and

possibly booting up computers, opening apps, or preparing tools or instruments.
- **The last 5-10 minutes:** You're cooling down, losing steam, beginning to lose focus and energy, starting to wonder about the next task, packing things up, summarizing, and winding down.

It stands to reason that if you have, say, five distinct hour-long blocks in a day, then all together that's ten periods of warm up and cool down, amounting to a staggering *50-100 minutes* of time lost to "context switching."

That's one whole hour. It adds up: Over the course of a year this amounts to more than 300 hours of precious time that, once gone, can never be recovered.

It certainly shines a new light on the "not enough time" claim!

By **batching your tasks** and **theming your days**, you reduce time lost to context switching. For example, if you choose instead to do the same task (or the same kind of task) for five combined hours, then the time lost to context switching drops to just 10-20 minutes total.

It's not just time you're saving, you're also saving energy and focus. Every time you switch tasks, your focus and momentum leaks away and you find yourself feeling a little more fractured. This explains that feeling that the day is made of a thousand stressful pieces that somehow don't add up to a single win. Batching and theming can help!

How do you do it?

- **First, consider all your tasks and task types**
    - Make a list of all the activities you tend to do in a week
    - Try to categorize all tasks down to a set of themes or types, for example: "admin", "writing", or "emails"
- **Next, block off time for each theme**
    - Schedule a time in your day where you can focus on this theme and this theme only
- **Finally, factor in your energy levels and deadlines**
    - Make sure you're assigning your most important and most demanding activities for when you're feeling most alert, usually in the mornings
    - Plan according to deadlines and around other fixed commitments

To give an example, you might be an entrepreneur. Let's say you identify several different tasks you need to do in a typical week, like:

- content creation
- marketing and promotion
- networking and relationship building

- research and professional development
- client work
- managing finances and general admin

You might decide to make Mondays your Networking and Correspondence day. You block out this time to catch up on emails and messages, reach out to people, catch up on industry news and maintain your network. These are all different tasks, granted, but they fall under the same theme or type, so the switching cost is minimized.

Then, Tuesdays can be your bookkeeping and finance day, and Wednesdays can be your dedicated client work day, for example. You could work on a career development course on Thursday in anticipation of grading and feedback occurring every Friday.

Within each themed day, you can further organize yourself so that the hardest tasks are done before noon, and the more routine ones later in the day, once your focus and energy levels have dropped a little.

Block Your Priorities Weekly

Your time blocks are not made of stone.

It's a guide, not a straitjacket.

At the start of each week, dedicate 15-30 minutes to scheduling your time blocks. Instead of just leaving important tasks to float around on a To Do list, be proactive and identify those things that are likely to be most urgent and impactful in the coming days. Then block them in.

Now you're in control.

Life happens, and so your system needs to be flexible enough to accommodate the unexpected, without sacrificing your output.

Observe, assess, and adjust. Then observe again.

Repeat.

What if a task takes longer than I planned? If you've reached the end of your time block but not the end of your task, don't worry.

- If you can, continue to work until the task is complete and reschedule anything coming after.
- If you can't, stop the task and reschedule the rest for later.
- Either way, take careful note so that you make more realistic allowances next time.
- Make a note to revisit your overall strategy the next time you're scheduling your week.

What if I keep running out of time?

- The honest answer? You're likely overcommitting or overestimating how much you can do.

- You'll need to adjust, but be careful about where the adjustment will come from:
    - You can do fewer tasks or less work on a task
    - You can find a way to work harder, faster, or quicker
- Here's the thing though—if you want to do more on a certain task, you'll almost always have to do less on some other task, or do fewer tasks overall. It's a tradeoff; but you get to choose which direction to take it.

Remember: If you're not using your time, you're losing it.

Time blocking isn't about cramming in more. It's about using time deliberately and making space for what matters.

Chapter 4: Find the Why Behind Your Tasks

"We work to become, not to acquire."

- **Elbert Hubbard**

What are your goals?

Most people can easily list off the things they'd like to have:

- "I want to buy a house within 3 years."
- "I want to complete my degree."
- "I want to save $100,000."
- "I want to launch my own business."

These are all things that we *acquire*—objectives we achieve and add to our lives.

You've probably already heard of SMART goals, i.e., that a good goal should be Specific, Measurable, Attainable, Realistic, and Time bound.

However, simply setting a goal and achieving it is not the whole story. The whole story needs to include an answer to the question, "But why?"

You want to launch a business. But why?

You want to save $100,000 or buy a house or get a degree. But why?

Unless an action is connected meaningfully to a purpose, then it is just noise and movement.

Goal setting is very important. However, goals are secondary and instrumental—they're there to serve a purpose.

"I want to save $100,000."

"OK. Why?"

"Because I want to be more financially secure."

"Cool. But why?"

"Because... that just seems like something I should be doing?"

Without a purpose, your goals will be groundless and circular. Why do you want to achieve your goals? In order to achieve your goals. Having $100,000 just sitting there certainly means you can tick a box. But, much like money, goals aren't really worth anything until you *do* something with them.

Are you saving for a more comfortable retirement?

Do you want to start experimenting with investing so you can work less and create a passive income?

Do you want to spend more time with loved ones?

It can be difficult to admit that, on closer inspection, you're not that clear on what you actually want, and why.

You may find yourself in a tricky position:

- You're not totally motivated or inspired
- Your tasks seem pointless or boring
- You feel aimless and lost
- You're going through the motions but it's exhausting
- You're confused and have decision fatigue
- You procrastinate and have lost your zest

One possible reason: Your goals, and the tasks connected to them, lack a meaningful *why*.

Another way of looking at this dilemma is the way Elbert Hubbard does: **We need to carefully consider who we want to become as people, not just what we want to acquire and achieve.**

If you know why you're doing something, it's far, far easier to summon up the courage, energy, and enthusiasm to do it. You have a reason to push past fear and laziness, and you have a clear picture of that end point that you truly desire.

If you don't know why you're doing something, everything will feel like a slog.

Tasks become boring, distractions become irresistible, and your productivity tanks.

You might still be taking action, but your action lacks impact.

You may get lost in busywork, stuck giving the impression of effort, instead of making real effort.

You may fail to prioritize, take on too much, then burn out.

Without a clear internal "why," you rely on external pressure to get things done—deadlines, guilt, or urgency—and that's not sustainable or enjoyable.

But when every task has a reason behind it, even mundane work starts to feel like it matters. Challenges and setbacks are tackled because you know why you're tackling them, and no matter how bored or tired you feel, zooming out to remember the bigger picture can quickly restore your motivation.

Here's how to ground yourself in deeper purpose.

Tie Tasks to Personal Values or Outcomes

When you look at items on a To Do list or the title for a time block, you could be forgiven for thinking that tasks are just standalone obligations. Just things you have to do.

Push back against this sense of arbitrariness by regularly reminding yourself of how these tasks fit into the bigger plan—no matter how small they are.

- Why does this task matter?
- What are the consequences of doing this task?
- Where does completing this task lead me?

- What does this task ultimately support?
- How does this task help me become who I want to be?

If tasks seem random, unconnected, and pointless, it's natural that you'd unconsciously resist doing them.

If you can see what they're for, however, how they help and in exactly what ways they move you forward, it's far easier to apply your sustained focus and energy.

Make a habit of rewording tasks so you can see the purpose baked into them:

Instead of "meeting, 3PM" phrase it as, "chat with Janie to discuss partnership possibilities/build new relationship."

When you see tasks as instrumental in this way, as ultimately **helping you become the person you want to be**, then you cannot help but be more interested in them.

Ask, "Why Does This Task Exist?" During Planning

If you're routinely feeling lackluster about your tasks, it may be that you need to rewind even further and consider why you've assigned yourself that job in the first place. Ideally, this should be done as you're planning for the week or month ahead.

How often have you assigned yourself a task just because... well... it seemed like the kind of thing you should be doing?

This is precisely the kind of task you will end up procrastinating, dragging your feet, and wasting time on!

Ask yourself: **"Why does this task exist in the first place?"**

There are two possible outcomes to this line of questioning:

1. **You appreciate the value of tasks, even small ones.** You realize that even a seemingly mundane chore, like reorganizing a filing system or submitting legal paperwork, serves a valuable purpose. Even if you don't enjoy the task, you can appreciate the value it brings, for example: It saves you time later, prevents bigger problems down the line, or opens up better future possibilities.
2. **You realize that certain tasks actually *don't* have a reason to exist.** What a relief! Instead of trying to force yourself to be productive doing a task that shouldn't exist in the first place, you can just drop it and re-evaluate.

If something doesn't connect to your broader, overarching goals, and if it doesn't materially bring you closer to being the person you want to be, or to living the life you want to live, then it doesn't belong on your To Do list.

It doesn't deserve any space in your head, either.

Review Weekly to Reconnect with Meaning

At the end of each week, take a little time to review and reflect on the tasks you've completed.

It's not just about "moving the needle." It's about feeling that that movement *means* something and matters in the bigger picture. Over the course of the last week:

- Which tasks felt the most worthwhile to you?
- Which tasks felt the most energizing?
- Which tasks felt pointless?

For every task that you've achieved, see if you can identify not just the raw output, but the direction and purpose of that output. You're not just doing a *quantitative* appraisal, but a *qualitative* one. For example:

"Presented new onboarding flow → helps new hires get integrated faster → goes toward creating a cohesive company environment, which I care about."

You may need to draw a clearer line that connects:

- Your values, purpose, and broader intention (big picture)
- Your goals (medium picture)
- Your daily tasks (small picture)

Or you may discover that a daily task does not in fact connect to your goals, or that one of your goals does not connect to your higher purpose or values, in which case you can safely let it go.

When you know your *why*, your *how* becomes easier, more focused, and more productive.

Tasks stop being items on a checklist, and start becoming steps towards a meaningful, value-based goal. You become powerful, purposeful, and intentional... not just busy.

To put it another way, you are *becoming* productive, not just *acquiring* productivity.

Chapter 5: Say No to Overloaded To-Do Lists With 3 + 2 Rule

"A slow sort of country!" said the Queen. "Now, here, you see, it takes all the running you can do, to keep in the same place. If you want to get somewhere else, you must run at least twice as fast as that!"

- *Through the Looking Glass,* Lewis Carroll

The term burnout was coined as recently as 1974, and yet today, it seems like every other person is—or will soon be—burnt out. People are worn down, exhausted, and disillusioned with the sheer amount of work their daily lives demand from them.

The answer is not to do more meditation, self-care, or therapy. It's not to do more of anything at all. Instead, one obvious low-hanging fruit is to consciously choose *not* to overload yourself with an enormous To Do list.

The solution is to do less.

Hustle culture has taught the lesson that productivity means amping up effort: if you want more, you do more. The belief is that if you just push harder, you'll finally catch up one day and earn yourself some rest.

The truth is not so black-and-white. Many people all over the world are effectively held in slavery by a bloated To Do list. They constantly feel bullied, hurried along, watched over, and nagged by a list that never semes to get smaller.

- They feel busy but strangely stuck at the same time.
- They know they should progress, but somehow they can't.
- They're overwhelmed, even though they've done "nothing" all day.
- They cross an item off the list but it doesn't matter, because another item instantly appears in its place…

If this sounds like you, don't worry. You're not lazy, you're *paralyzed*.

The symptoms of task paralysis include cognitive overload, irritability, confusion and loss of focus, fatigue, impaired mood, and, ultimately, burn out.

While breathing exercises and vacations can be temporary bandages, the problem will continue to return if the root cause is never addressed.

And what's the problem?

A To Do list a dozen items long, plus all its psychological consequences!

First things first: Of course it's smart to have a list of tasks, and to stay organized. However, if we just impulsively put every thought and idea on our To Do list we can quickly end up with something that makes us feel exhausted, hemmed in, and stuck.

Enter the 3+2 rule, which is a more realistic, streamlined, and *humane* approach to making a To Do list. It's simple: You focus each day on three major tasks, add in two minor ones to keep your momentum and motivation up and call it a day.

That's it.

The way out of burnout and task fatigue is not to add even more tasks. It's to start hacking away at the inessential, and to start cutting ourselves some slack. The irony with this approach is that ultimately, you'll get more done, and you won't have to deplete yourself in the process.

- No more cramming.
- No more scrabbling to clear the list no matter what.
- No more guilt and shame and dread at leaving items undone.

Instead, you make your To Do list on *your* terms and narrow your focus while conserving your energy. You keep activities manageable and sustainable, make progress visible, and acknowledge and celebrate small wins.

An overloaded To Do list is not a badge of honor nor a sign of dedication. It's not something you owe the world and it's not proof of your value, commitment, or capability. It's not a magical talisman nor a slavedriver that you have to answer to.

It's time to kick To Do lists off their pedestal and trim them down to size. The 3+2 method helps you do just that.

Choose Three Major Tasks That Drive Progress

The Japanese have a system of industrial scheduling they call *kanban*, and it's an approach that has been variously adapted to the workplace and to the accomplishment of personal goals.

Unlike the conventional To Do list, which can theoretically grow to any size, the *kanban* approach depends on setting limits.

It's the difference between identifying a ceiling and compiling a wishlist.

You decide what the upper bound is for the number of tasks you'll work on during the day, and that's it—you do not add another task until you've finished one. You don't even think about it.

Essentially, you have a fixed number of "works in progress." If this number is, say, three, then you should never be handling more than three open tasks at any one time. If you complete one of those three, then you can take on another task.

Create a card: Make it small—smaller than you think. This is your new To Do list. Write your three main tasks on this card and promise yourself that you will not add anything more to it. Tomorrow you'll make a new one.

If you like, you can have a "waiting" list where you queue tasks, but this may drift into To Do list territory, so is best avoided if you're just starting out.

What counts as a major task?

- They take around 2 or 3 hours to complete
- They contribute meaningfully to a goal
- If you were to complete them all, you'd feel like you had a successful day

Focusing on just three main tasks may feel a little scary or counterintuitive at first. But this feeling could just be a hustle hangover. You may feel antsy for a while. Like you're not doing enough. Like there are 20 ultra-important tasks that you're neglecting…

But stay with it.

Accept your finite capacity.

Do the work that you can do today, today, and let the rest go.

The truth is that you really can't do a thousand things at once, no matter how much you think you should. Increasing demands on yourself will not change that fact, and may even slow you down.

The secret to overcoming burnout is this: Understand that at any one time, you have to choose which activity you'll pay attention to, and which activity simply has to wait.

That's all there is to it.

The burnout pattern is to open a task, work on it, open another task, work on that a little, open another dozen tasks, and have all these unfinished bits of business hanging over you at all times. As a result you feel trapped and depleted, as though a thousand little devils were always trying to get a piece of you.

The productivity pattern is to open a task, complete it fully, then move on to the next. As a result you feel calm, focused, and fulfilled because you're closing those loops, one at a time.

The world may demand that you juggle a million things at once, but that doesn't mean you can or should attempt to. There's no point holding everything in your head unless you can take meaningful action on it, and you can logically only ever take meaningful action on one task at a time. So do that.

Choose your three main tasks, and take a deep breath.

You don't have to achieve everything all at once.

Just these three.

Add Two Quick Wins for Momentum

Next, pick two small tasks that will only take 15-20 minutes to complete.

You want to choose tasks that are relatively easy and quick, so that you can create a boost of both momentum and motivation—but without losing too much energy.

If you feel terrorized by your own To Do list, it may be because every item on there is big, gnarly, and complicated. You're dreading starting those tasks because they're complex and require an enormous time commitment. When you're already feeling exhausted, seeing these outstanding tasks is likely to make you feel totally disheartened.

Your three main tasks are where the bulk of your energy goes.

Your two small wins are there to maintain momentum and give you a dopamine boost between bigger tasks, or when you're catching your breath and resetting your focus.

Small win tasks can include:

- Writing and sending an email
- Tidying and organizing
- Scanning and summarizing a paper
- Making a quick call
- Making a payment or sending an invoice

- Completing a form
- Proofreading a document

For quick win tasks to really do their job, make a point of actually celebrating them. Pause and acknowledge your progress, even if it's small. Then imagine yourself using that little burst of motivation to keep you going.

Stick to the Card, and Let the Rest Wait

The 3+2 method's beauty is in its simplicity.

Three big tasks, two smaller ones, and that's it.

You'll notice some overlap here with the 1-3-5 approach we discussed earlier, and indeed they are similar. The main difference is that the 3+2 method is more about crafting a focused and streamlined To Do list from scratch, whereas the 1-3-5 method is about clarifying for yourself what is and isn't important, from an existing list.

Another big difference: You'll notice that for the 3+2 method, there isn't any room allocated for trivial, unimportant, or unnecessary tasks.

What if I finish my list early?

- Pause to reflect and evaluate
- Celebrate your accomplishment
- Or just take a break!

Resist the temptation to start loading up the list again—there will be time for that tomorrow.

What if something urgent comes up, and it's not one of my three major tasks?

- Take a deep breath, and relax.
- Identify whether this really is *urgent* and *important.*
- If it's important but not urgent, or urgent but not important, revisit your list tomorrow and consider setting it as one of your three tasks.
- If it's urgent and important, consider whether it genuinely displaces one of your current tasks, and *choose* to replace it if so. Act, don't react.
- If it's neither important nor urgent, you know what to do: ignore it.

We are the only ones who can reduce our own mental clutter, protect our energy, and draw boundaries around our time and effort.

Most of us have good reason to blame the modern world for leaving us overwhelmed and overworked. On the other hand, nothing can capture our attention or steal our energy without our consent.

One of the best ways to reclaim your own inner resources is with a more intelligent To Do list.

You don't need a longer To Do list. **You need a To Do list that matches your energy level and respects your limits.**

Stay grounded and realistic in what you can do, and paradoxically you'll progress faster—and feel more satisfied about the progress you do make.

Chapter 6: Slump Mode Protocol

"There is a vitality, a life force, an energy, a quickening that is translated through you into action, and because there is only one of you in all of time, this expression is unique."

- **Martha Graham**

We've all been there. Perhaps you're there right now.

You can't exactly say why, but you're *just not feeling it.*

It's not that you suddenly hate your job or that you've changed your mind about everything.

What's a slump day? It's zero flow. It's being decidedly *not* in the zone. It's any day where you experience:

- Low motivation
- Mental fog
- A feeling of slowness and heaviness
- An inability to get started
- Boredom
- The sense that everything is harder than normal

This is not the same as overwhelm or burnt out. It's not anxiety or laziness. It's more about what's *not* there—your sparkle.

Firstly, cut yourself some slack. Everyone has the occasional slump day, and it's perfectly normal.

Slump days can sneak up on us when we're feeling tired, under the weather, or just misaligned.

You may be in a slump because you didn't sleep well the night before, because your body is dealing with something, or because you've just come out of an intense stretch of work.

Slump days happen.

There's no need to beat yourself up.

There's no point fearing the lull or trying to force your way out.

You don't need to panic that something's going badly wrong.

But when that fog hits, you *do* need to change things up.

If you can pre-emptively devise a Slump Mode Protocol, then you'll be prepared to meet sluggish days head on. The idea is to *gently* help yourself reset and refresh. You want to get yourself feeling right as soon as possible, without getting sidetracked by judgment or guilt.

Below is an easy protocol that you can try as is, or else use as a starting point in the creation of your own protocol. It has three simple steps:

1. **Wake up your physical body**
2. **Fire up your curiosity**

3. Take action

The great thing about this protocol is that it doesn't require enormous amounts of energy—which if you're in a slump, you won't have. Instead, you give yourself a little grace and take a few simple steps to get moving and flowing again.

Let's take a closer look.

Start With the Body

There's a reason that the word "slump" so accurately describes this state of dull inertia—it's usually not just a mental and emotional condition, but a *physical* one.

Have you literally been slouching and sagging?

Your body and your mind are not two different things; they're two different expressions of the same thing. If you're feeling dull and lifeless, chances are that you've allowed yourself to grow physically stagnant.

It's a chicken-and-the-egg situation, but we're not concerned with whether the body is influencing the mind or the mind is influencing the body. For our purposes, all we need to know is that **moving the body is a reliable way to get the mind moving**, too.

Increasing physical movement:

- Boosts blood flow

- Boosts lymph flow (i.e. increases your body's ability to clear away its own waste and metabolic byproducts)
- Releases mood-boosting endorphins
- Fires up your nervous system
- Activates your muscles
- Helps your tissues to oxygenate

All of these things tell the body: "We're awake!"

Movement acts like a reset button. You're like an Etch-a-Sketch that gets given a good shake so you can start over.

You don't need a full workout to send your body and brain the *wake up* message, however; you can also simply:

- Stretch for five minutes while breathing deeply
- Go for a short but brisk walk
- Do a one-song dance break
- Get into some vigorous housework or chores
- Do some jumping jacks or a sprint with your kids

Even something as simple as changing your orientation in space can wake up a sluggish body. Move around. Stand up, sit down cross legged, twist from side to side, or wiggle your fingers.

Wake Up Your Curiosity

Now that you've woken your body up a little, try to channel all that life and vitality into a specific direction.

Consider this: Why do people feel lackluster about things in the first place? It might not be because of overwhelm, but it's exact opposite, boredom and stagnation, In other words—a lack of stimulation.

Some people make the mistake of interpreting their own slump moods as fatigue. They reason that they need more rest, but somehow the rest they take doesn't refresh them. Why?

Because they weren't tired to start with. They were *bored*.

There's no spark in your world because there currently isn't anything to make it spark! Think of your slump state as a signal your body is broadcasting: "I'm waiting for something to capture my curiosity."

We are back to the *why* question.

If something feels pointless, we simply won't care about it that much. That not-caring-much state of mind is *not* tiredness, it's a yearning for meaning. It's hunger for a spark of interest.

You can certainly reinvigorate yourself by remembering the deeper *why* behind your tasks, but this may not always be enough. You may need a little extra something to re-convince you that the world is an interesting place, filled with interesting things worth getting stirred up about.

How?

- Give yourself permission to just... follow your nose
- Forget about "should" and just pay attention to what seems genuinely interesting, fun, or mysterious
- Move in the direction of those things that pique your interest—can you learn more?

Don't worry if the interest is only small or brief, or if the subject material doesn't seem immediately legitimate.

If it fires you up, arouses your interest, or gets you to sit up and pay attention, then allow your curiosity to be sparked. The trigger doesn't have to be relevant for you to value the spark it provides.

For a moment just let yourself play and discover, no agenda needed. You may be surprised just how much energy appears to come out of nowhere!

- Read an article that really makes you think and wonder.
- Watch a video that has you full of questions and responses.

- Stop merely asking yourself a hypothetical question and try to find out the answer in earnest.
- Notice a novel thought drifting across your awareness and just engage with it, scribbling and doodling down your ideas.

Two big caveats here:

- **Chasing spark is *not* about productivity.** There's no need to pretend it is. You're not trying to do any heavy lifting here; you're just flipping the light switch on and getting things moving again.
- **Following curiosity is not about digital distraction**. Falling into some mind-numbing screen-based activity is not it. You're looking for that *self-initiated* moment of true curiosity—not passively turning up to an algorithm and asking it to give you direction.

Pick One Anchor Action

Your body has been given a refreshing jolt, and so has your mind.

Now it's time to get the train back on the tracks so it can start moving again. Action connects you back to the world of cause-and-effect and plugs you back into the momentum of your tasks. Importantly, it is *your* unique action because it comes from *you*—from your life force, your passion, and your energy.

You don't have to tackle your entire To Do list at once or achieve some grand accomplishments—just start.

Pick one thing that feels doable right now.

Something low-effort and low-stress.

Something small enough to pick up without dread and heaviness, but big enough to give you the feeling that you're moving ahead *on your terms*.

For example:

- Sending a small email
- Throwing away something that's been sitting around your desk for ages
- Compiling a shopping list
- Making a decision about some minor errand
- Paying a small bill online
- Mailing a parcel
- Responding to a message
- Catching up on some low-level correspondence

It doesn't really matter what the small task is; it's merely acting as a trigger or runway to more meaningful tasks.

Once the engine is no longer cold and you're building the first bit of momentum, one thing leads to another, and you're officially out of your slump. From there you have other resources to draw on.

To reiterate, when you're in a slump:

1. Don't beat yourself up, or go into guilt and shame
2. Get your body moving
3. Look for the spark and follow it with curiosity
4. Take small, easy actions

You can tweak this process according to your own preferences and tendencies, only take care to avoid pressuring yourself to take massive action, or to grind your way through something that feels tedious—you'll just create more friction and resistance.

Use the Buyback Loop to Break out of Inertia

Every single task you do either *takes* energy or it *supplies* it.

Very few tasks are completely neutral.

Some tasks grind you down, others light you up.

Some eat up time, life force, and money, and yield very little in return, while others are net gains.

Some bring enormous amounts of tension and chaos into our lives, others bring clarity, ease, and focus.

Slump days are normal. But if you're *routinely* finding it difficult to sustain energy and motivation, you could have a bigger problem on your hands:

- Too many activities of the wrong kind
- Too few activities of the right kind of

OK, that might be oversimplifying things, but if you're spending the bulk of every day on activities like pointless emails, boring calls, paper-pushing, and low-impact admin, then it's no surprise that you'd feel uninspired.

Occasional slump days need our self-compassion and flexibility.

Chronic and recurrent slump days? That's more like a red flag.

Ignoring this red flag and pushing through the slump is playing a lose-lose game. You'll only be burning out the best of yourself on tasks that just don't matter.

Take persistent slump days as an invitation to reassess:

- Am I working hard or smart?
- Am I spending most of my time on those activities that are most profitable and most fulfilling to me?
- Am I wasting time on tasks that only have minimal payoff?
- Am I sacrificing my passion?

- Am I thinking only in terms of money or box-checking, and neglecting to factor in my energy, emotions, and purpose?

Your slump may be nature's way of telling you that your current system is wasteful.

Whenever there's a slump, there's usually an energy leak. What's draining you?

There is a helpful system called the Buyback Loop, which is a method for auditing how we spend our time. We consciously work to remove low-value tasks from our days so that we can "buy back" that time and invest it in something that actually matters.

It's about identifying and patching up those leaks!

We give the tasks that we dislike or can't do very well to others who do like them and can do them very well. Sometimes, we eliminate tasks entirely. The energy and time we save can then be re-invested elsewhere—like in all those things that fire us up.

The system is a *loop*—it's not a one-and-done phenomenon, but an ongoing and iterative adjustment process:

- **Audit** – Identify those low-value tasks that are sapping energy/motivation.
    - What tasks do I hate or dread?

- - Which have minimal payoff and leave me in a slump?
- **Transfer** – Give those tasks to someone else (or otherwise automate or systematize)
  - Who else can do it? Is there someone who will enjoy this task?
  - Is there someone I can pay or negotiate with?
- **Fill** – Take the space you've opened up and fill it with higher-value tasks
  - What really brings joy, profit, and impact into my life?
  - How can I do more of that?
- **Repeat**
  - The process is an ongoing loop of refinement.

Here, high value activities are any activity that generates money, that has high impact, or that brings spark, interest, and passion into your world (or all three).

We will revisit the Buyback loop in many different shapes and guises throughout this book. For the purposes of this chapter, though, we're interested in how slump feelings can actually be a useful metric for how we're budgeting our energy and enthusiasm.

Chronic slumps may be caused by too many energy-sucking tasks that are not bringing you enough of a return. Offload these tasks and upgrade the way you use your time so that new energy and purpose flows in again.

Moments of discomfort, boredom, or dullness can be flashing neon signs pointing to a lack of alignment. **Don't force your way through recurrent slumps—learn what you can from them and then engineer them out of your life.**

Chapter 7: Consolidate Repetitive Tasks Using the DRY Principle

"Efficiency is doing better what is already being done."

- **Peter Drucker**

This next tip comes to us from the software development world: **Don't Repeat Yourself.**

Redundancy is a killer, and it's often an invisible drain on your time, energy, and money.

In *The Pragmatic Programmer* (Hunt and Thomas, 1999), we are told, "Every piece of knowledge must have a **single**, unambiguous, authoritative representation within a system."

This is the DRY principle, and for our purposes, we can replace "knowledge" with "task."

To be productive, every task must have a **single**, unambiguous, authoritative representation within our system.

We already know that busyness is not the same as efficiency.

Just because we're active and moving doesn't mean we're getting things done or moving forward in any way.

The DRY principle is not just about *doing* something once and only once, it's about how we *represent* that task in our system. If every task requires hours of rumination, writing, planning, thinking, and organizing, then guess what? You don't have single, unambiguous representations anymore.

What you've got is mental clutter.

Sometimes, the feeling of unfruitful busyness is really just a sign that you're being redundant and repeating yourself.

You're writing the same email over and over.

You're fixing the same thing that keeps breaking in the same way.

You're completing the same bit of admin again and again.

It's not that you have too many tasks, it's just that you're doing the same task more times than it needs to be done.

The DRY principle encourages us to ask:

- What can I eliminate?
- What can I delegate?
- What can I automate?
- What can I consolidate?

Software engineers are lazy. Like most of us, they prefer solutions that yield the highest output for the least input: instead of writing the same bit of code again and again, they find a way to write it *once*, then make shortcuts that refer back to that snippet when necessary.

You don't have to be a coder to build this principle into your own daily schedule, which is, after all, a kind of system.

Identify and Batch Your Repetitive Tasks

The first step to cutting down on repetition is to get a clear idea of where it's happening in the first place.

That means **tracking all of your daily activities for a fixed period**—a week is a great place to start, but a month is better.

If it takes time to do, then log it. Everyday tasks, unexpected activities, emails, scrolling, admin and maintenance, reading, *everything*. You are not looking at the best-case schedule you set for yourself; you want to see where you're actually spending yourself:

- Your time
- Your energy
- Your enthusiasm

Where is it going? How much duplication do you have?

Try not to analyze or interpret anything to start—just gather the data.

Once you've gathered at least a weeks' worth, start looking for patterns.

- **What tasks seem to be on repeat?**

- For example you may be answering the same queries on a loop, filling out the same form or going through the same sequence of administrative steps.
- **What tasks do you dread and resent?**
  - This is just a gut feel—flag those tasks that leave you feeling slumpy and annoyed.
- **Which tasks usually tend to hold up and delay everything else?**
  - Maybe there's always a step in a procedure that needs someone else's approval, or there's a bottleneck that always stops up a good workflow.
- **What tasks really guzzle your time?**
  - Look for those things that always take longer than you anticipate.

If a task is repetitive, holds you up, is time-consuming *and* leaves you feeling drained, then it's a good candidate for DRY treatment. You may find just one or two offenders, or enough different tasks that it's worth batching and categorizing them.

Build Repeatable Systems with SOPs

Once you've identified points of redundancy that are costing you time and aggravation, you can start "coding" a better way.

Unlike with an actual computer, your Standard Operating Procedures (SOPs) may be a little more abstract, and require some careful forethought.

An SOP = step-by-step instructions for how you will complete each task.

Keep it simple. You're building a kind of machine to help you replicate tasks with minimal effort—not something so complex it requires additional maintenance.

SOPs should help you move faster, make fewer mistakes, and reduce stress and distraction.

What does an SOP look like? Here are some examples to give you an idea:

- You notice you keep writing the same email over the course of a month → you create a template or a few template variations that you can tweak, cut, and paste as necessary.
- You notice that you often field the same inquiries from clients → you compile a master FAQ list or info sheet to point them to.
- You notice that you go through the same sequence of steps using certain apps and web pages → you build in shortcuts, bookmarks, and autocompletes.
- You notice that you spend a lot of time sending and managing invoices and proposals → you find an app or tool to take care of it for you, so you can focus on the easy parts.

- You notice that you're often worried about making certain payments and recording them in your books → you set up a direct debit and have it automatically updated on your bookkeeping system.

Delegate or Outsource When the System is Solid

If you build a solid, efficient system, then it no longer requires your close attention, which means that pretty much anyone can watch over it.

In the previous section, we discussed the Buyback principle and how delegation can save you time that you can then put to better use. However, you want to be careful about *what* you delegate.

1. Identify redundancies
2. Automate or systematize
3. Delegate

There is an art to delegating with confidence.

Delegation is *not* handing over the reins to someone else.

Delegation is taking the reins more firmly in your own hands, while someone else takes care of everything that might get in the way of that.

Whether you opt for a teammate or a virtual assistant, **you are never handing over tasks; you're handing over systems.** You are not dumping busywork on someone, you're outsourcing the maintenance of a proven system.

Invest time and energy in creating this system, then step back and let it start recouping a return for you in both time and energy.

Repetition and redundancy are leaks—time, money, energy, and attention are frittered away. A good system, however, ensures that you do a task once, you do it unambiguously, and you do it with authority.

This will make life more streamlined, more consistent, and more predictable.

A Word on Unnecessary Tasks

We opened this chapter with a quote from management theorist Peter Drucker, but we can imagine that this sentiment comes with a caveat: **"Nothing is less productive than to make more efficient what should not be done at all."**

Take a good look at your repeated tasks and **ask whether the problem is that… you're not facing the problem**.

For example, every time you leave your house through the front door, the side panel on the door comes loose and needs to be nudged back into place again. This nudging procedure takes about 20 seconds and you do it *every single day,* often more than once.

You are repeating yourself.

You are wasting your time.

But, you'd waste even more of it if you contemplated at length how you might improve the nudging. Could you wiggle it back into place a little faster than normal? Could you shave the 20 seconds down to 15?

This is a tongue-in-cheek example to illustrate the ridiculousness of trying to streamline a task that should never have existed to start with. You do not need a new SOP here, or a better SOP. You just need to get rid of this task once and for all!

That means fixing the panel, or removing it so there's nothing to break anymore (a third option: choosing to no longer be bothered by the out-of-place panel).

Be ruthless:

- Does this task need to be done at all?
- Is this task recurring because an underlying problem is not being addressed?
- Is there a single high-effort solution right now that would spare me endless low-effort patch-ups in the future?

Nothing is quite so satisfying as taking action that releases you from the obligation to keep taking action. We'll be taking a closer look at this idea in our final chapter.

Chapter 8: Avoid Zero Days

"It does not matter how slowly you go as long as you do not stop."

- **Confucius**

Pop quiz: What is the *biggest* reason that people fail to achieve their aspirations?

   a. They lack ambition
   b. They lack intelligence and/or ability
   c. They don't work hard enough
   d. They don't want it enough

Actually, it's a trick question. People can fail to reach their goals for all of these reasons. They might fail because of all the things they lack, and all the things they don't do.

But perhaps the *biggest* obstacle is the opposite of what we think it is; perhaps people fail *because they collapse under the weight of trying to do too much, too fast, all at once.*

In other words, they fail not because they don't do enough, but because they burn themselves out chasing big wins, impressive accomplishments, and dramatic overnight transformations.

To put it yet another way, *not doing enough* often comes as a result of pushing ourselves to do *too much*.

It's not glamorous, but **consistency wins out over intensity**. Every time.

Compare the following stories to see exactly how this dynamic plays out:

Story 1

1. You set a big, audacious goal
2. You take impressive action and make progress
3. You hit an obstacle
4. You wobble a little, then stall
5. You have a full-on bad day. You don't take the action you should and you're disappointed
6. Another day where you don't take action
7. You throw in the towel
8. You're back at square 1

What causes your big goal to fall apart here? It's not step 3, the obstacle. It's step 6, deciding that the obstacle, and your subsequent mess-up, warrants your abandonment of the entire project.

Let's look at an alternative.

Story 2

1. You set a big, audacious goal
2. You take impressive action and make progress
3. You hit an obstacle

4. You wobble a little, but instead of stalling, you take a decidedly less impressive action
5. You take another unimpressive action, but you're still going
6. You regain your speed and pick up again
7. You continue on the path
8. You repeat steps 2 to 7 until eventually you achieve the goal

The difference here is what happens at steps 4 and 5.

Your action here may well be disappointing, and less than you'd like. But it's *something*.

The No Zero Days principle is about loosening the psychological expectation for perfect performance every single day. It pushes against black and white thinking: "Either I do this really well all at once, or I don't do it at all."

If you are content with incremental progress, humble baby steps, and small, consistent wins, then you are less at risk of seeing small mistakes and slip-ups as a reason to stop.

The philosophy is simple: **Never allow yourself to have a Zero Day, that is, a day where you take zero action towards your goal.**

This way, you keep away from all-or-nothing thinking and stay instead within that crucial middle zone.

You don't demand high performance every day, but you never permit zero performance, either.

Life happens, and sometimes you don't hit your quotas, reach a milestone, or perform in exactly the way you'd like.

So what?

If we have unrealistic expectations that we have to do *everything*, then we risk burning out and giving up.

But if we allow ourselves to do *nothing*, then we risk losing momentum and motivation entirely.

The No Zero Days rule is about working with occasional obstacles, lulls, and setbacks, without resorting to perfectionism.

It's the middle way.

Do One Tiny Thing (No Matter How Tiny)
Think progress. Not perfection.

Move the needle, even if it's just a teeny tiny bit.

When you're unwell, having a slump day, or dealing with the unexpected, you may not be able to do what you set out to do. Sometimes, your *only* option is imperfect, incomplete, and unimpressive action.

Take that action anyway and keep moving.

Even if your entire day felt unproductive, it's not too late to make it count. It may be 11:59 p.m.

and you haven't done a useful thing all day. That's OK. Take that final minute to write a sentence on your report, do 10 sit ups, or tidy up one tiny bit of clutter.

It's OK if it's a low day, a slump day, or a disappointing day. Just don't let it be a Zero Day.

Sometimes, the size of the action doesn't matter as much as *the fact that you made it.* Show up, do the work, and try again tomorrow. That's all. You're going slowly, but you're going.

Tomorrow, it'll be easier.

Pick One Goal You Can Chip Away at Daily

You've come down with a bug.

Something unexpected came up.

There's a minor emergency which has thrown all your plans out the window.

When you're having an off day or things just aren't going to plan, the last thing you need is to be scrambling around trying to conjure up energy you just don't have or create time where there simply isn't any.

- Identify a clear long-term goal
- Brainstorm up to ten mini actions that are modest, but still move you forward
- When you're having an off day, go to your list and pick something

If you plan ahead in this way, then there won't be any need to overthink or angst over what you should do when stuff goes wrong. You'll already know what to do. And that inherently takes the pressure off.

Can't do the whole report?

Then just do a paragraph.

Can't do a paragraph?

Then just do a sentence.

Without laboring the point, if even a sentence feels impossible, then do a single word. As long as it's *something*, it will maintain a sense of psychological momentum. You're still in the game. You're still showing up.

Some days that may not feel like much, but it counts.

Adjusting your mindset to fit your circumstances

Remind yourself that modest, sustainable actions are always preferable to grand intentions that start with a bang… but then quickly fizzle out. It may *feel* like you need big, impressive action to move forward, but in a way this is just another distraction.

The truth is that success is usually achieved not with exciting quantum leaps, but with the slow accrual of unremarkable baby steps. Stay on the path and take that baby step.

Many of us hold unconscious beliefs about the *form* productivity has to take in order to be legitimate. We believe that work only counts if it looks like complicated time management systems, endless "deep work", continuously breaking our own records, and carrying out punishing morning routines day after day.

If and when you can do that heavy lifting, great. But some days? You need to be honest about what you can do and find a way to make that count.

Log Your Progress Where You Can See It Grow

With the No Zero Days mentality, you start to **prioritize momentum.** You start to value unbroken strings or chains of consistent action, rather than single episodes of epic action.

With the No Zero Days approach, you are not exclusively fixated on the upper limit and how much you can achieve; you're also factoring in the lower limit, and the bottom standard you will not allow yourself to fall beneath.

Essentially, **you're setting your default**: Even at the worst of times, you are never inert, never disengaged. You allow yourself to have down days, but you *choose* what the lowest energy day looks like.

This is not just about keeping a psychological sense of still being in the game. It adds up in a real way. Let's look at a little example.

Let's say you're writing a novel, and you decide to never let yourself go to sleep until you've written at least one paragraph, i.e. 200 words or so. That's your default, lowest-energy state.

→ Doing the math, this means that *even if you have nothing but bare-minimum days for an entire year*, you'll still produce 365 x 200, i.e. more than 70,000 words. That's the length of an ample sized novel.

Read that again: It is possible to achieve your goals even if you do nothing but what you decide is your bare minimum.

On the other hand, imagine that you set yourself the ambitious-sounding goal of doing 2000 words a day, because that seems pretty productive, and your ego likes the sound of it.

Some days you achieve this 2000, and on rare occasions you're in the zone and do more. But then on slump days, or days you're ill, or days when something else important comes up, you find that 2000 words is basically an impossibility.

Now what?

You lose consistency. Some days you hit it out of the park, other days you lose the plot entirely and, filled with guilt and shame, you do nothing. Sometimes, this "nothing-streak" goes on for days… or weeks. Maybe even months.

→ Doing the math: if you had "productive" 2000-word days every single day, you'd complete your novel in less than two months. But what if you maintained this productivity level only for a week, and then spent the next 12 months managing a 2000-word day here and there, interspersed with months of shame-filled zero days? At the end of the year you'd have *half* a novel (assuming you didn't lose interest entirely and give up within a month…)

Again: You can push yourself to have "productive days" and still underperform.

The secret ingredient is consistency. Nothing flashy.

If you plodded along writing just 200 words a day, you'd barely break a sweat. You'd never quite reach the point of needing to force yourself, or call in the big willpower guns. You'd coast along on *habit*, knowing that your bare minimum will always keep you moving.

However, when you're caught in the all-or-nothing cycle of productivity-then-crash, you're not just less productive, you're also more strung out. You never acquire the writing habit, so every word is a new negotiation, a costly decision requiring effort and will.

It's a stressful way to work. And it *doesn't* work.

One way to center momentum over intensity is to **cultivate winning streaks**.

To do that, you need your day-to-day progress to be visible. You need to *see* the slow but steady accumulation of your goal. How?

- **Monitor yourself.** Use a journal, a note-taking app, a Google sheet, a habit tracker, a wall calendar, or plain old paper and pen to observe your small wins slowly adding up to big ones.
- **Stay motivated.** The longer the chain becomes, the more motivated you are not to break it. Any small action keeps it going. Breaking the chain just doesn't feel worth it.
- **Keep it low stakes.** You're not counting what you do; you're just logging every consecutive non-zero day.

Small steps toward your goal may be so small that you cannot really perceive them day to day. By making them visible, and adding every small action to the growing pile, you build momentum and remind yourself that yes, even though it doesn't always feel like it, small actions *do* count.

A meaningful step in the right direction always counts, no matter how small, because it's always better than zero.

No need for massive action.

No need to get overwhelmed.

No need to feel guilty for all the epic things you didn't quite manage to pull off today.

"But what if actually have a Zero Day?"

Well, so what if you do? Just because you have one, it doesn't mean you have to have two. Wake up tomorrow and start the streak again. Shame and guilt may pop up, but they will do precisely nothing to get you back on track again, so you may as well let them go.

Work with what you have today. Never allow a low-ebb day to become a zero day… and even if you *do* fall to zero, never allow a single zero day to snowball into a nothing-streak.

Make your default minimum non-zero, and don't beat yourself up if you need to fall to that level now and again. Tomorrow, try again.

Chapter 9: Use a Single Source of Truth

"For every minute spent in organizing, an hour is earned."

- **Benjamin Franklin**

The rather grandiose term "Single Source of Truth" or SSOT actually refers to a very practical and intuitive method for staying organized.

SSOT is originally a management term that broadly refers to **all relevant information stored in a single, centralized place.**

There is overlap here with the Don't Repeat Yourself principle—the single source speaks authoritatively, unambiguously, and *once* concerning any process, procedure, or question.

If you have several bits of redundant information spread haphazardly all over the place, you're repeating yourself.

A SSOT can be:

- A literal giant file containing important documents
- A sprawling series of digital folders on Google Drive
- An internal wiki
- A project management app
- A static repository of contracts, templates, spec sheets, etc.
- It could even be, in some cases, an actual person

Whatever form it takes, the purpose of the SSOT is to provide anyone in the organization with the "truth." This guarantees efficiency, clarity, and immediacy.

How does this apply to productivity, especially for those of us who are working towards personal goals?

If you've ever wasted precious hours looking for a lost document, got confused by your own folder system, or found yourself duplicating information in error, then you may need an SSOT—even if you're just a company of one.

Essentially, **the worse your organization, the worse your productivity**. You'll be wasting time navigating the system itself, rather than using that system to achieve the goal it was created for.

Scattered information silently kills productivity. Every minute you spend bumbling through various apps, folders, notebooks, sticky notes, and scribbles, you lose momentum. Those losses add up fast.

- You forget things.
- You get sidetracked or pulled into irrelevant rabbit holes.
- You crumble under information overload.
- You experience brain fog, decision fatigue, and confusion.

- You get muddled when it comes to appraisals and decision-making.

Many of us think of disorganization almost in an aesthetic sense—just something we might do to maintain a superficial sense of order and control.

But organization goes much, much deeper than this.

Our organization reflects our priorities, our mindset, our habits, and our values. The way we organize ourselves (or not, as it were) is a manifestation of the *seriousness* and *clarity* that we bring to our endeavors.

Our degree of organization influences the speed and efficiency with which we reach our goals:

- Without good organization, we cannot **think** clearly
- Without clear thought, we cannot **act** with power or focus
- Without focused, powerful action, we don't **achieve** our goals

A clear central hub to coordinate all your disparate ideas, thoughts, tasks, bits of information, research, and ideas is both cause and effect of *single-mindedness.*

If we hope to transform our ideas, plans, and knowledge into concrete accomplishment, then we need to draw a single, clear line connecting them all.

The SSOT's value lies not in its complexity but in its simplicity. No fancy rules necessary.

Build Your Personal Command Center

The first step is to figure out the shape and format your SSOT will take. You could opt for a cloud-based storage system, software, or note-keeping app, or go old-school and use pen and paper and hard copies in files and folders.

It depends on:

- Your preferences
- The nature of your goals
- The volume of information you need to centralize
- The nature of that information

You could choose something like Google Drive, Evernote, Notion, or even a tool or system of your own design.

Within this system, create a series of subsections or subfolders. For example, you could include:

- Goals
- Reference notes
- Ongoing projects
- Weekly priorities
- Banking information
- Yearly plan
- Study materials

- Templates
- Schedules
- Workflows and SOPs
- Videos and presentations
- Receipts and invoices
- New ideas
- Research catalogue
- Contracts
- FAQs
- Passwords, security information
- Important numbers

Remember that this process may take a little trial and error, and your SSOT may look quite untidy before it starts to look organized. But try to view this process itself as clarifying—you are uncovering existing areas of confusion and redundancy.

Your system may be many levels deep and require quite a sophisticated hierarchy, or it may be more relaxed and free form. Just remember to let the information lead, rather than trying to force it into a system that it doesn't fit.

Label It So Even Future-You Gets It

Once you've created the basic architecture of your SSOT, you need to start thinking about how you'll navigate it.

Your system will be useless unless you can quickly find exactly what you're looking for. The best way to do this is with a clear, logical tagging system.

Name every bit of information in a consistent way so that you can quickly find it at a glance.

Less useful names:

- "Brain Dump" (what on earth could be in *there*?)
- "Ideas 4" (how do they relate to Ideas 1, 2 and 3?)
- "20/08/2025" (this is just a date... but why is it important?)

More useful names:

- Summer Budget 2025
- Content Ideas Reels
- Bank Statement July 20

Spare a thought for your future self and name things in a way that makes it crystal clear what every document or piece of information is about. You don't just want to reflect the information in the document itself, but how it relates to other pieces of information.

So, if you have a huge collection of different content ideas, you may have:

- Content Ideas Reels
- Content Ideas Static Post
- Content Ideas Blog Post
- Content Ideas YT Script

If you carelessly name one folder "Ideas for Content FB" then it won't be stored with the others and will be harder to find. It needs to be named "Content Ideas FB."

As you can see, **organization is a way of encoding your own process**. It's effectively an SOP as discussed under the DRY principle—you decide where a piece of data fits *once* and then you never have to waste time figuring out where it is again.

The idea is that future-you will be able to find what they're looking for even if they're tired, grumpy, or it's been 6 months since they last thought of this material. Your system should always be doing the work for you.

Maintain the system

Another aspect of this "organizational encoding" is to have a protocol for the maintenance of the system itself:

- Whenever you create a note, acquire a piece of information, or generate useful data, have a routine for how you embed it into your SSOT. You may like to have a kind of "inbox" or staging folder where you place items that require processing and filing.
- Keep your devices synced up and make sure that you're making regular updates.
- If you discover an expired, incorrect, or misfiled piece of data, immediately rectify the situation and make the necessary tweaks. Your organizational system is a

living entity and will grow and change over time.

Always Check the Source Before You Think Again

How many times have you solved a problem only to realize that you'd actually already solved this problem once before, and just forgot?

Often, we launch into fresh fact-finding or data-gathering without realizing that we already have the information at hand.

Don't reinvent the wheel every time you have to put together a plan or make a decision. First double check your SSOT to see whether you haven't already tackled this issue before.

It's a small habit that:

- Saves you time that you might have wasted on rediscovering knowledge you already have
- Prevents you from duplicating that knowledge and cluttering up your system—this benefits your future self

You don't have to start from scratch as often as you think you do. Even if the complete answer is not available, you might be surprised to discover a bunch of relevant information you'd forgotten about—information that makes the process of finding new information far easier.

The less time you spend gathering yourself, the more time you have to actually get things done. This is the power of a well-designed SSOT at work!

Chapter 10: Maximize Your Downtime With Time Pockets

"The bad news is time flies. The good news is you're the pilot."

- Michael Altshuler

Back in the day, women made quilts. This was done out of necessity: Fabric was scarce and expensive, so instead of wasting little offcuts and remnants, every tiny piece was salvaged and patched together to create something entirely new. Those enterprising women of the past understood a fundamental truth: **Even scraps have value.**

We can do the same thing with our own time—which is after all the most precious resource, since we can never manufacture more of it.

Enter the idea of using "Time Pockets," which we can think of simply as scraps of time left over after the main sections have been cut off and set aside.

A Time Pocket: Any small, unused piece of time in the day, usually falling between other scheduled tasks and activities.

These little remnants of time are everywhere, once you start looking for them:

- Waiting for the microwave to ping
- Hanging around between meetings

- Realizing you finished a meeting early and are at a loose end
- Waiting for your coffee to brew in the morning
- Waiting for the mechanic to finish looking at your car
- Sitting in a dentist's waiting room
- Waiting for someone who is late for an appointment
- Commuting
- Waiting for the tumble dryer cycle to finish
- Being on hold on the phone
- Standing in a queue
- Waiting to pick your kids up from school

Yes, these little Time Pockets are pretty insignificant in themselves. Just like fabric scraps, though, their value lies in saving them up and creating something bigger with them.

Use these time scraps well and you can stitch up more productivity, better mental health, and an overall improved state of flow through the day.

What can you do during a Time Pocket?

Ideally, this time can be used to quickly dispatch an errand, chip away at a bigger task, or go for a quick win that doesn't require your full or prolonged attention.

This is a path to boosting productivity that simply requires you to use what you already have, but are not consciously choosing to use.

No need to do more. Just salvage what would otherwise go to waste.

Now, having Time Pockets in your schedule is not a problem or a sign of poor planning.

They're also not something we should deliberately seek out.

Instead, they're like those fabric scraps—unavoidable and incidental.

With a little forethought, you can be *prepared*, and make sure that you're ready to snap up these Time Pockets as and when they occur.

Keep a Five-Minute Task List Nearby

Important: Not every single spare second of time needs to be crammed full of intense work.

Being more productive with spare bits of time doesn't mean creating a schedule of back-to-back effort. It's more a question of being aware of where your time is going, and choosing to put it to your use, rather than letting it evaporate.

Short and trivial tasks can be annoying to stay on top of ordinarily, but they're a perfect match for Time Pockets. Compile a list of mini-tasks for this purpose, i.e., tasks that take around five minutes to complete.

This could be:

- Sending a short reply to a message
- Scheduling an appointment

- Double checking some fact or detail
- Making a reservation or confirming times and places
- Printing out and filing a document

Or, if you work from home, little pockets of time can be used to stay on top of those household chores that would otherwise steadily pile up on you:

- Packing or unpacking the dishwasher
- Laying out your clothing for the following day
- Folding laundry
- Tidying up surfaces
- Organizing counter spaces

You could even use Time Pockets to make small investments in your relationships and social life:

- Checking up on someone you haven't connected with in a while
- Sending a sweet message to a loved one
- Making a social plan for the evening or weekend
- Making a kind gesture to show someone you're thinking of them
- Checking to see if any birthdays or anniversaries are coming up

Whenever you find yourself with unexpected free time, immediately go to your list (perhaps you have it stored in your SSOT!) and quickly tick one off the list.

Whatever you do, don't fall into the automatic scroll habit. If your smartphone is a confirmed time waste trigger for you, consider setting your quick task list as a wallpaper or background so you see it the moment you pick up your phone.

What if a task takes less than five minutes?

Do it immediately. Managing and processing extremely small tasks takes more energy than it does to simply do them. If something can be done in a few minutes, do it right now. Don't give it a second chance to hang around and take up space in your mind.

Break Big Projects into Bite-Sized Actions

For Time Pockets that are longer than two minutes—say ten to fifteen minutes—you can plan ahead in the same way as above, and list out slightly longer tasks such as listening to a podcast or reading a book.

You could also **identify a large activity and break it into smaller, more manageable chunks**. That way, whenever you have a free moment, there's a list of small, easy tasks you can do at the ready.

If you wait until you're in the Time Pocket to scramble around and find something meaningful to do, those minutes may evaporate fast, and you'll have achieved little—except maybe to have frustrated yourself.

For example, imagine you have a report to write, and it's a task that will take you roughly two hours. Before you even begin, you plan ahead and chop the task into several ten-minute blocks:

- Clarify central argument
- Decide on main headings
- Compile outline and decide heading order
- Write introduction
- Write conclusion
- Etc.

You may use time blocking to schedule this task for a particular date and time. However, until that time comes, this task can be considered open and fair game for tackling during unexpected down times.

When a friend messages to tell you they're running fifteen minutes late to your coffee date, whip out your phone—not to scroll aimlessly, but to quickly tackle one of these smaller chunks.

If you make this kind of thing a habit, it's a little like leaving money in your wallet for your future self to find. When the scheduled time block arrives, you may be pleased to discover that you've already covered a lot of ground.

For example, you immediately get engrossed with writing the main body of the report, because all those little Time Pockets have added up to a clearer sense of what you need to do.

Nibbling away at bite sized tasks really adds up.

- The momentum is already there
- You begin the task with a store of accomplishment already in place
- There's less to do, which means you can do more with the time you've allocated

The more you can practice this kind of **opportunistic flow**, the more cohesive your day will feel. It may seem counterintuitive, but proactively using spare bits of time in this way can make a day feel lighter, less rushed and more rewarding.

Use Kanban to Chip Away at Tasks

A Kanban board is an organizational method that's especially useful for keeping track of Time Pockets.

For those unfamiliar with Kanban, the approach is simple. You **make or buy a whiteboard that is divided into three or four columns:**

Backlog	Work in Progress	Validate/Review	Complete

You then populate the above fields with sticky notes or cards and magnets that each represent a single task.

Every task begins in the very far left column, then, as though through a pipeline or conveyor belt, moves through the columns, in order, until it's complete.

To apply this to Time Pockets, consider making each card or sticky note a small or medium sized task that you expressly intend to tackle in your spontaneous free moments.

When all the cards or sticky notes from a big task land up in the final column, it's complete. Hooray!

It can be extremely satisfying to see finished tasks slowly pile up in the final column—knowing they got there without using any additional time.

Compare that with the measly return you get from mindless social media scrolling!

Other tips and tricks for making the best use of your time scraps:

- Keep a folder of interesting articles and papers that you'd like to read, but don't normally have time for. Every time you're at

a loose end, read a page or two. Ditto for educational videos.
- Keep a "question book" or file where you scribble down ideas, random thoughts, and things you'd like to investigate further.
- Do a brainteaser or log a few minutes in a language learning app.
- If you're studying or preparing for an exam, polish up on your learning by reproducing an important diagram, formula, equation, or chart from memory.
- Make a shopping list or pre-emptively see if there are any chores or errands you can do now before they become urgent.
- Take a moment to do a micro-workout: a quick walk, a stretch, or some yoga.
- Do a little environment scan and check if something needs tidying, fixing, topping up, or de-cluttering. Scrub off that stain you've been looking at for weeks or get rid of that ancient stack of papers at last. Order more hand soap. Fill up the tank. Tidy up that top drawer.
- Finally, don't forget the most obvious use of a random Time Pocket: a break. Get some fresh air, meditate or say a prayer, chill out, get a snack, or chat with a friend. Important: Screen time is seldom truly relaxing.

Chapter 11: Destroy Time Craters

"Tell me to what you pay attention and I will tell you who you are."

- Jose Ortega y Gasset

Earlier, we discussed the sneaky leaks that happen around time blocks, i.e., those hidden warm-up and cool-down activities that cost us time and energy.

Context switching and multitasking expand that margin around tasks and allow waste and inefficiency to creep in.

The ratio of fluster : deep work rises.

Your productivity drops.

The same principle applies when it comes to distractions and interruptions: The effect of a two-minute disruption can actually be much, much bigger than just those two minutes.

Time craters: Small interruptions with outsized consequences.

Asteroids can be tiny, yet when they hit earth their impact is so immense they can leave craters ten, twenty, or even thirty times their size.

The Vredefort Crater in South Africa, for example, is the largest impact crater on Earth, and was formed more than 2 billion years ago. The asteroid in question was just 10-15 km (around 6–9 miles) in diameter, whereas the crater it produced is estimated at a whopping 300 km (around 190 miles).

So what does a *time* crater look like?

Like this:

- You check your phone when you should be focused on a task
- You see a new message in a WhatsApp group chat
- You quickly post a short reply
- You put your phone away and carry on with the task

Doesn't look like much, right? Total time is just 30 seconds or so.

But that's just the asteroid. Now let's look at the crater that asteroid causes:

- You're working on your task but you're *thinking* about whether anyone found your reply funny
- A few times you glance at your phone again and wake up the screen to see if there's any notifications
- You spend some time mentally drafting a few more funny messages
- You check your phone again
- Occasionally, this checking results in you getting caught up in your daily feed, checking

the weather, or going to your favorite time-wasting sites
- Now you're thinking about all *that*
- You check your phone again
- Something happens and before you know it you've wasted a half hour reading some garbage online that you don't even vaguely care about
- You finally return to your task.

That 30 second distraction? It's paved the way to a 30-minute time sink and a whole load of distracted, shallow work.

The distraction is a problem, but you're usually distracted for far, far longer afterwards than you may be aware.

- You may take a break in the office to guzzle a giant caramel Frappuccino with extra cream and sprinkles. It only takes ten minutes to wander over to the café and drink it, but the resulting sugar crash lasts for *hours*, and puts an end to that work flow you had going.
- A bit of mindless doomscrolling may take just five minutes of your time, but the resulting agitation and low mood destroys your productivity for the rest of the day and casts a long shadow over everything you do.
- You keep thinking of an exciting date you have coming up that evening. The date itself will likely be just an hour long, but you can't

think straight for the entire day leading up to it.

A little distraction here or there can completely derail a day. The damage is seldom in the distraction itself ("It's only five minutes!") but in the consequences, and the time lost to recovery.

You may feel that you've pulled back your attention and returned to a task, but if you're still thinking about the distraction, anticipating a future distraction, or trying to regather your composure, you're only experiencing a kind of illusory productivity—fauxductivity, if you like!

Until you start appreciating the *impact* of distractions, and not just their size, you won't be able to take appropriate action and reclaim your day.

Watch Out for Sneaky "Small" Distractions

Time to be honest with yourself.

Your "harmless" distractions may actually be blasting enormous holes through your day.

Do a realistic accounting of the *total effect* a distraction is having on you.

- Consider the loss of time and the disruption to mental flow and clarity
- Consider the cost of context switching
- Consider the time needed to settle down again and return to your previous state of mind

Every distraction temporarily increases your distractibility—no matter how small you think it is. If there are enough "small" distractions hitting you from all sides, it may feel like you *never* get a chance to actually sit down and work.

What to do?

Be ruthless.

You already know which mindless distractions you need to avoid—things like social media posting, reading the "news" or browsing low-value forums for memes.

Unfortunately, there are no easy, low-effort ways to resist these temptations.

- If possible, remove the distraction from your environment entirely. It's harder to be distracted by something that just isn't there
- Try to build in more rewards on your own terms to reduce reactivity and keep you motivated in a more meaningful and connected way

It is important to note that not all distractions are the same. Your daily life may be filled with fake wins and distracting busywork that feels important, but isn't.

Is it really that important that you clear your inbox?

Reply to that comment?

Read that article?

Sometimes the most damaging distractions are those that sneak in under the disguise of real work.

But ask yourself: "What is my most important task for today? Does this thing add value to that task in any way?"

If not, consider it a distraction. Then move right along.

Build a Barrier Around Your Focus

Finally, remember that **distraction isn't always external.**

The distraction crater is often a mind-made phenomenon. Maybe we quietly agree to allow our attention and interest to be hijacked by some thought or feeling. Maybe we make ourselves just a little too available so that when a distraction hits, it meets with a willing accomplice who's ready and waiting.

Don't cultivate a state of mind that is "distraction waiting to happen."

Don't be available—mentally or emotionally—to tasks that you have not explicitly committed to.

That means putting firm and clear boundaries around your time and attention well *before* something appears to violate them.

- Close your office door

- Close all browser tabs and the entire browser itself if you're not using it
- Keep your inbox out of your sight
- Turn off the TV or radio
- Put your phone on silent
- Put up a Do-Not-Disturb sign
- Turn off notifications
- Wear noise-cancelling headphones
- Where possible, do not agree to instant email replies and having 24/7 availability

Tell yourself:

My time is not public property.

My energy is mine and it's for my use.

My first act of free will is to decide where to place my attention.

Use Visual Anchors to Stay Grounded

Geological craters are a spatial margin around an impact.

Time craters, on the other hand, are created by *temporal* drift—i.e., the margin of time that forms around the impact of a distraction. Some examples:

- You forget what you're doing.
- You switch to another task.
- From that task you drift again, onto the next task...

You don't know it but you're leaving a trail of unfinished business in your wake.

Not only does this kind of temporal drift slash your productivity and weaken your focus, it's also *uncomfortable*. Have you ever ended a day feeling wired and as though you cannot switch off?

That's your brain telling you that it can't rest because there are still too many outstanding tasks open on your mental desktop. You can't *remember* those tasks, but their incompletion may still leave you with a vague sense of uneasiness.

Let's be honest: Distractions do happen and even the most focused among us will find our minds wandering now and then.

But you can minimize the size of that margin. You can reign in the drift.

How?

By using visual and physical cues to anchor your time and stay grounded. Think of these cues as literal anchors—they're like time checkpoints in your day that prevent you from drifting too far. Here are some ideas:

- **Use a Timer.** The minutes and hours can easily drift simply because you can't *see* them. You suddenly realize an hour is gone, but you didn't feel it going. Make time visible

and set yourself mini deadlines so that you're more conscious of how you're moving through time.
- **Clocks**: Position one in your line of vision. Even better if it's a digital clock with large numbers, or an analog clock with an easy-to-see second hand, so you can get a real grounded sense of one minute passing to the next.
- **Mini-deadlines**: Loosely map your activities onto small time segments, for example break up an hour work session into five minute chunks, each of which is assigned a mini-task. Keep checking in with the clock to stay on track. You'll still be tempted to distraction... but the resulting crater will be much smaller!
- **Keep an "Idea Book."** Intrusive thoughts, random ideas, and spontaneous musings are normal, but they can be doorways into rabbit holes that soon lead you far away from your intended task. You can divide your book into different sections:
  - **Worry list**: Write down concerns and anxieties instead of letting them lure you off your mission. Tell yourself you'll come back to them later, at a time of *your* choosing. The truth: Most worries "expire" after a day or so anyway.
  - **New ideas, reflections, and interesting questions**: Same principle. You can process them later, at the right

time, and integrate them into your SSOT, or else block out deliberate time to investigate further.
- **Tasks, request, and demands**: Create a queue for tasks and, if they're frequent, consider strengthening your boundaries or creating a redirect; for example, an automated email reply or text response.

Time often drifts because we have the feeling that if we don't chase this particular distraction the very second it appears in our field of awareness, it'll float off again and we'll lose it. When you write things down this psychological tension is reduced:

"Thanks for bringing this to my attention, brain. I've made a note now, so I won't forget. You can stop reminding me now."

One interesting side effect: You may notice that some of your productivity tools and apps are actually the biggest culprits for distraction and time wasting. If something is distracting you, diluting your efforts, or fracturing your attention span and mood, *make it less visible.*

The distracted mind treats every new stimulus like an irresistible compulsion. Attention becomes like a paper boat—flimsy and liable to be thrown around by even the tiniest ripples in the water.

Reverse this tendency: Anchor your chosen task in the real, visible world, and make the distraction feel ephemeral, unreal, and insignificant.

Chapter 12: Say No With the Hourglass Method

"The art of leadership is saying no, not saying yes. It is very easy to say yes."

- **Tony Blair**

Let's extend our consideration of the question of distractions.

When you work, you're pouring your mental, physical, cognitive, and even emotional resources into a task of your choosing—a goal-driven task that your higher self has decided is meaningful and valuable.

You are deliberately channeling your enthusiasm, energy, and awareness in a single direction.

A distraction is an intrusion on all this.

A distraction says, "Hey, can I siphon off some of that good stuff for a task that is less valuable? Less meaningful?"

The disciplined mind can usually answer: "No, of course you can't!"

In this way, being focused, disciplined, and productive is essentially choosing to say NO every single moment of every single day. The thing you say YES to represents the tiniest sliver of your universe—everything else must take a back seat.

Unless you can say no effectively, you will never be able to:

- Safeguard your time
- Stay focused
- Protect your resources
- Maintain momentum

If you find it difficult to say no to *internal* distractions, then *external* ones are also likely to be a problem.

Have you ever quickly agreed to a request, only to regret doing so later?

Have you ever impulsively acquiesced to someone's demand, when on second thoughts you really should have declined?

Essentially, a spontaneous request or demand is a *distraction*. Nothing more.

Juliet Funt is founder of a boutique efficiency firm, and author of *A Minute to Think*. According to Funt, these "flash responses" are driven by many things:

- A culture of hustle, heroism, overwork, and urgency
- A belief that our default state should always be to comply
- An attitude that others are (at least partially) entitled to our time

Funt has devised a technique to counter this stance, and it's called the Hourglass Method. The key to this approach is to **intentionally slow down and buy yourself enough time to make strategic, mindful decisions.**

The idea is that you run through the consideration process *on your own terms*, rather than merely reacting to external pressures.

1. Retreat
2. Carefully consider the request
3. Choose confidently

Whether you decline or accept is irrelevant—the point is that you are the one who is consciously choosing what to do, so that you are always fully aligned with your true priorities.

Here's the process in more detail.

The Hourglass

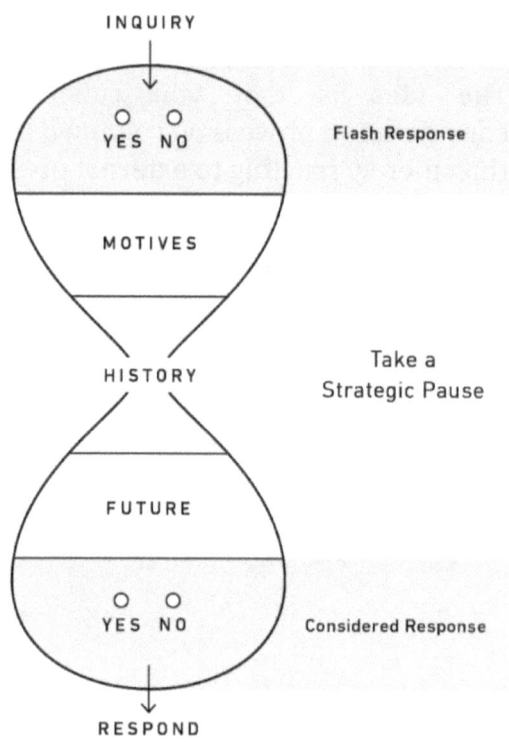

Credit: Juliet Funt

Step 1: Note Your Flash Response

If you're a chronic people-pleaser or used to disregarding your own boundaries, you may have taught yourself overt time to ignore your initial response to requests.

Let's say someone emails you out of the blue, calls you up, or pops their head round your office door and asks something of you.

The first crucial step is to **ask for a little time**. Get into the habit of never giving immediate responses—this will take some practice.

You don't need to retreat and mull over the question for years, just politely ask for a moment and then consult the hourglass.

Become aware of the flash impulse you first had when the request appeared: **What was your instinctual response to the request?**

Try not to overthink this. It's just a yes or no thing. Important: This is not what you think you *should* feel, but what you actually feel.

- Calm willingness?
- Dread?
- Annoyance?
- Anxiety?
- Reluctance?
- Eagerness?

Step 2: Take a Strategic Pause

Now take a moment to work your way down through the rest of the hourglass, i.e., spend a little time in consideration.

In turn you will consider:

- Your motives
- Your history
- Your future

Let's open each of these up:

- **Your motives.** Why did you have the initial reaction you did? Be as honest as possible—you're the only one who sees these notes.
    - Are you trying to people-please, placate, take responsibility for, or impress someone?
    - Is your reaction one of fear—like you're trying to dodge certain repercussions or avoid conflict?
    - Are you indirectly hoping to be liked, praised, or needed? Perhaps there is a martyrdom element.
    - Might you actually be willing to be called away from your current task and diverted to something less challenging/unpleasant?
- **History.** How have similar experiences played out in the past for you?
    - When you said yes to a request like this in the past, what happened?
    - When you said no, what happened?
    - What is your normal tendency with this kind of request, and how is that working out for you so far?

- **Future**. Think ahead and consider the repercussions of your response to this demand. Look beyond the present demand and consider others that may come after it.
    - How will agreeing now impact your future goals?
    - How will disagreeing impact you?
    - How will your choices and attitude now influence your responsibilities and sense of self in the long term?

Though this may look like a lot, you can move through the hourglass fairly quickly. Smaller and less significant requests won't need longer than a few minutes, while more important requests will naturally take a little more time to unpack.

Remind yourself that people are allowed to make requests, and that you are allowed to carefully consider them.

Own the process. Don't rush.

Step 3: Give a Considered Response

Once you've reflected on things for a while, you'll find yourself drifting down to the very bottom of the hourglass. You are now in a position to answer in a way that is:

- Considered
- Responsive not reactive
- Confident

It would be a mistake to suggest that saying no is always the best response.

There has been a rise in the self-help and productivity world of a misconception that there is something almost sacred about the word no—to the extent that many people say no in just as kneejerk a fashion as they previously said yes.

It doesn't matter whether you say yes or no. What matters is *why* and *how* you say these things, and to what end.

The Hourglass Method makes space for self-honesty in both directions. You might, after all, be tempted to say no and convince yourself it's because you're being proactive, focused, and disciplined. The truth? You're lazy and would like a convenient excuse to shirk a genuine responsibility.

Many people are chronic yes-men, stuck in the habit of over-accommodating, people-pleasing, and consistently leaving themselves out of the equation.

Others are consistently selfish, uncollaborative, and insincere, all while using the language of boundaries and self-care to wriggle out of reasonable expectations others have of them.

Only you know which one you are! The Hourglass Method can help you work through your own reasons in a considered way, and start to find a balanced compromise between your own path and the path the outside world would like to steer you on.

Let's finish off by considering a few practical phrases you can use in everyday life.

How to ask for more time:

- "Hey, can I get back to you on that?"
- "Let me look at my calendar and give you an answer later this afternoon."
- "Hm, I'm not sure. Let me confirm a few things first and I'll follow up with you at tomorrow morning's meeting."

It may feel awkward to ask for time in this way at first, especially if you're used to jumping immediately to fulfil every request.

If your reply is polite and prompt, though, then you will still come across as receptive, and as though you're taking the request seriously enough to actually consider it, rather than just blurting out an agreement.

Remember: You can be polite, helpful, and responsive even if you don't acquiesce immediately.

How to decline a request:

- Give a reason: "I appreciate you coming to me for help, but I've had a look at my existing commitments, and I'm going to have to pass this time."

- Point to a limited resource: "I'm afraid I can't, sorry. I just don't have the time right now."
- Provide an alternative or negotiate: "I'm not available in January, but I do have some openings in February, if that might work for you."
- Simply say no: "I'm sorry, but no."

Wording matters here, as does your nonverbal communication. While it's polite and considerate to add in an "I'm sorry" or "unfortunately", you don't want to go overboard.

Why? You may give the impression that you're just dying to comply, only there's some circumstance out of your control that's preventing you. This means that if you're up against a very persistent or desperate person, they may find a way to helpfully remove your excuse, leaving you feeling forced to comply or else be extra blunt.

Keep it short and sweet.

Be polite; let your tone of voice, body language, and word choice reflect kindness and cooperation even though you're firmly declining.

An example:

Let's say you're at a parent teacher meeting. The class teacher spontaneously asks if you'd be interested in volunteering to be part of a committee to oversee a new summer school program. You had vaguely expressed a willingness to help last summer. Everyone in the room turns momentarily to see what your response is going to be, and you suddenly get a bad case of stage fright.

Quick—the first step is to buy yourself time.

"Ooh, I'm flattered that you considered me, that camp is such a good idea. Can I just check in with my calendar first and come back to you this evening?"

Paired with a smile and warm body language, the pressure is off of you.

The next stage is to make a quick note of your initial response. Thinking back, you realize your instinctive reaction was overwhelm and a sense of being put on the spot. Indeed, sometimes people unconsciously make impromptu demands like this in public, since they can feel almost impossible to turn down.

You take ten minutes or so to work through your motives, your history, and your future. You note down:

- **Motives**: With brutal honesty, you know that your initial reaction was unwillingness, but that you're feeling pressured to say yes because you don't want to be judged for being an uninvolved or uncommitted parent. Looking further, you realize that there is no

innate desire to agree—you'd just be doing so to save face.
- **History**: You recall how you've already overcommitted once before in very similar circumstances. You felt good for all of five minutes, and then spent months feeling resentful.
- **Future**: Not only do you consult your calendar and check whether you actually have the time resources available, you're aware that saying yes now sets a precedent.

You politely decline later that evening.

"While I know how important this camp is for some of the kids, I just don't have the time to do it justice this year. But I am happy to help with the fundraising raffle again."

Chapter 13: N.E.T

"Those who make the worst use of their time are the first to complain of its shortness."

- Jean de La Bruyère

This next technique comes to us from motivational speaker and personal development guru Tony Robbins. It's called NET:

NET = No Extra Time.

In short, it is possible to tackle all your meaningful projects, personal or professional development, reading, etc., in the little spaces of time that exist in the day you already have—no extra time needed.

This may sound strange at first.

Haven't most of us gotten into the habit of saying things like,

"Oh I want to [XYZ], but I just don't have the time!"

Whether it's reading important books, completing useful courses, learning a language or an instrument, improving our skills and abilities, or just taking time to work on ourselves, we seem to place this invisible condition on ourselves: *I can't do any of this unless I have extra time.*

The truth? You don't have that "extra" time now and you never will. Every day you wake up and you have precisely as much time as you did yesterday, and nothing you do in the world will change that.

Tony Robbins' idea, then, confronts this invisible excuse directly: If we hope to finally get around to the XYZ, then it has to be done now. We have to do it within an NET mindset, firmly acknowledging that there is no such thing as "extra time."

Important: The concept here is not about beating yourself up. Life really *is* busy. You're not lazy or crazy for finding it so, and you're definitely not alone.

Every open section of our calendars seem to be filled with:

- Paid work
- Commuting
- Life admin
- Errands
- Chores
- Emails
- Meals
- Family obligations
- Housework
- Exercise

We've already explored the power of identifying and exploiting everyday Time Pockets. NET works along similar principles: **We need to let go of the idea that there is some magical**

"extra time" that is coming to our rescue. Instead, we need to be realistic and get creative with the time we do have.

This is not multitasking.

It's not rushing.

And it's definitely not coasting!

It's simply about strategic time management and, more often than not, skillfully *layering* tasks. If you piggyback tasks on one another, you're making use of time that already exists, but you're just not using it to its fullest yet.

If you feel scattered and overburdened, the NET principle can help you do more with less. It's a low-effort, low-stress way to move forward, without making hours magically appear.

Here's how to do it:

Identify Daily "Autopilot" Time

First of all: Stop telling yourself you don't have enough time.

Realize that this is more often than not an excuse and a self-limiting belief.

You DO have enough time—if you can open your eyes and see where it is.

You can begin by doing a time audit on your daily, weekly, and monthly schedule. Look at all those tasks you do that keep you "busy" but don't necessarily require your full focus and brain power. This is autopilot time.

The time is certainly going, but you're spending it on fairly low-effort tasks that are not actually using you to your fullest:

- Walking the dog
- Doing your laundry, washing, ironing
- Commuting
- Walking into town to run errands
- Driving
- Showering and grooming
- Shopping
- Housework
- Running on the treadmill

Notice anything interesting here?

The things that we often feel eat up our time can actually be hidden *sources of time.* That's because when we're doing these things, our brains are largely free. This is not quite a Time Pocket, since we are doing something, but our brains are not required.

Once you've made a list of all the NET Time Pockets you have in your day-to-day life, pick just a few to start—you don't have to make major overhauls to your routine to begin reaping the benefits.

Be Conscious About What You're Listening To

Align the things you listen to with the person you actually want to become.

One of the easiest ways to make better use of autopilot time is to add an audio book or podcast.

What you listen to matters. Be intentional and choose audio that demonstrably moves you forward.

The truth is that lifestyle, health, wellness, and self-help podcasts are *everywhere* today, but very, very few are of good quality, and even fewer will be personally relevant given your unique goals.

If you're spending an hour listening to two random people talk about some obscure herbal supplement that you have no intention of using, you're not adding value—you're just stacking *two* low-value tasks on top of one another. It just becomes background noise.

Don't just listen to any old thing—be deliberate. Ask yourself:

- What's my current focus?
- What am I trying to achieve?
- What kind of person am I trying to be?

Let your answers inspire *intentional* audio choices that will support you.

Build a library of speakers and topics you care about, bearing in mind that just because you enjoyed a podcast by a speaker on one topic, it doesn't mean that you need to listen to everything they have to say.

You become what you think about, and you think about what you encounter most often in your world. So, take care when it comes to the kind of inputs you're giving your brain.

Don't listen to things at 1.5 speed and stress yourself out. Don't listen to speakers who rile you up and upset you for the same reason. Even if you agree with their *content*, their *delivery* may not align with your goals in a broader sense.

Remember that human beings end up reflecting and emulating the people they spend the most time with—and that includes digital people digitally! Take care about who you allow to influence you in such a profound way.

Tip: Spend a little time crafting a playlist so it's ready to go whenever you're in autopilot mode. Have your earbuds on hand and your device charged.

Tip: Review what you've listened to at the end of each week and celebrate any small wins and make necessary adjustments. Things can sometimes *feel* educational and inspirational in the moment, but after a few days have you thinking, "Wait what was the point of that?"

Keep Going With a Friction-free System

The last thing you want to do is saddle yourself with a mountain of additional decisions to make every time you head out to walk the dog or do your weekly shopping. You want to make your additional tasks happen as easily and automatically as possible, so that you're dialing up the value without increasing overwhelm.

- As before, create a playlist that you can just dive into, or consider longer audio books that provide hours and hours of high-value listening without provoking decision fatigue.
- Install a waterproof speaker in your shower so you can listen as you work through your grooming routine.
- Have several pairs of earbuds at strategic locations, like beside your bed or at the front door, so you don't waste time hunting them down.

The NET principle is about giving yourself more time to use, not more work to do, so make sure there are as few decisions between you and the task as possible.

While audio books and podcasts are brilliant for NET, with a little creativity you can identify a world of additional value-adding tasks.

- If you're busy with a very physical task, see if there's something you can do to occupy your brain

- If you're busy with a brain task, see if you can fit in some physical activity at the same time

Keep asking what tasks you can do together, without adding stress or losing accuracy.

Here's how that may look:

Your morning routine may begin with some meditation/prayer, journaling, and planning for the day ahead. You then have a shower but while you're doing so, you listen to a podcast or audiobook and start thinking about the day ahead.

Once done in the shower, you start brewing some coffee but instead of just sitting around waiting for it, you quickly feed the cat or do some quick stretches in the kitchen. While you're brushing your teeth you walk around the house and tidy up some of the kids' toys or put a load of laundry on.

You sit down in your home office (you work from home so you save all of that commuting time) and in the few minutes it takes for your computer to boot up, you give your desk a quick tidy up and start scratching together a three-item To Do list.

When the phone unexpectedly rings an hour later, you deal with it, but you immediately put the call on speaker so you can empty the dishwasher and start folding the laundry you put on earlier that morning. While dropping the kids off at school later you squeeze in another few calls in the car—a dentist appointment and a query about a family get together on the weekend.

In the afternoon you take the younger kids to the park and catch up on the news while they play, do a little mental meal planning, then right there on the park bench, you order your groceries online for delivery the following day.

That evening you do a YouTube workout (again, no need to waste an hour driving to the gym and back) and since it's a fairly brainless workout that doesn't require your full attention, you can mute it and listen simultaneously to any voice messages you've received during the day, or your audiobook.

Seen singly, all these little overlapped and layered tasks don't feel like much additional effort, but everything adds up. By the time you're done with your day, you have actually recouped an hour or two of "extra time" for yourself.

A caveat

Let's be real for a moment. Occasionally, "I don't have the time," is really just code for "I don't actually want to do this."

The time excuse is a way for us to avoid confronting a reality about our actual levels of commitment. So long as we can blame time limitations, we don't have to face our own fear, laziness, or doubt. We can hold onto the illusion that we would otherwise be super organized, accomplished, and fulfilled if it wasn't for our unfortunate lack of time.

If something is worth doing, then do it. Now. Don't wait for some ideal future time. Nobody is coming to give you permission or remove your obstacles!

Chapter 14: Monk Mode

"To produce at your peak level you need to work for extended periods with full concentration on a single task free from distraction."

- **Cal Newport**

Yes, "monk mode" is a cheesy TikTok trend, but at the same time, the principles it points to are timeless.

What *is* monk mode?

It may mean different things to different people. What pops into your mind when you imagine a monk? Perhaps it is someone who is:

- committed and single-minded
- masterful at deep work and focus
- ruthless with distraction and temptation
- self-disciplined
- purpose-driven and motivated by a higher good
- self-sacrificing and resilient
- restrained, temperate, and humble
- committed 100% to the cause

Whatever your conception of a monk, chances are it's *not* a lifestyle of mindless excess, digital distraction, careless immorality, low standards, general dissipation, shallowness, impatience, or triviality.

Perhaps there is a reason for the fact that, despite falling numbers of *actual* monks in the world, TikTok youth are rediscovering value in the propositions underlying the monk's way of life.

Productivity requires **discipline**.

It needs our **focus** and **commitment**.

It requires that we protect and direct our **attention**, that we conduct ourselves according to our higher principles and **values**, and that we take pride in serving something beyond mere sense experiences here in the present.

During the historical periods where religion was a more prominent feature of everyday life, monks were often the most educated, literate, and industrious members of their community. The historical scholarly, social, and scientific contributions of monks are hard to overstate.

To put it simply, monks have always known something about the art of *getting stuff done.*

How did they do it?

Define Your Monk Mode Boundaries

First, try to identify which (if any) characteristics of the monk lifestyle speak loudest to you.

- It may be the ability to retire from the world and put in long, uninterrupted hours of deep and meaningful work.
- It may be the ability to cultivate laser-like focus and concentration so sharp that you are unable to be distracted or pulled off course.
- It may be that rare, disciplined flow state that is only achievable when you genuinely, sincerely *care* about the goal you're trying to achieve.

It could be a blend of all these things.

Pick one monk-like attribute that you admire the most. What characteristic could use a little more development in your own life?

Once you've identified the monk trait you most desire in your own life, try to piece together a corresponding framework or structure onto which you can start hanging your daily routines. These things don't have to be big to make a big difference.

Some examples:

- **I want to be less distractable** – Set up blocks throughout the day when you are completely offline, notifications are turned off, and phones are silent.
- **I want to be more disciplined** – Establish a routine with yourself where

you get up every morning at 7 a.m. *no matter what.*
- **I want to be more focused** – Get into the habit of having just one main project to work on per day.

It doesn't matter what things you'd like to do when in monk mode (or the things you'd like to *avoid* doing). What matters is that the vision you're trying to bring to life is specific, realistically achievable, and aligned with the kind of life you're trying to create for yourself.

This may mean cutting or limiting social media, reducing the number of hours you spend online, gaming, or watching TV, drawing better boundaries around emails and messages, enforcing more regular wake and sleep times, tightening up your standards around exercise, diet, or housework, or simply paying more attention to your state of mind and stress levels.

Choose a Single Focus for Each Session

Relax—you don't have to burn your entire life down and start over! There's no need for major overnight transformations where you obliterate every tiny distraction and bad habit, while simultaneously rocketing your way into a superhuman state of perfect productivity.

In other words, you don't have to be a monk.

You can strategically use monk mode, however, as and when you need to.

Instead of striving to complete a 60-day self-improvement marathon where you tackle multiple areas at the same time, **choose just one point of focus, and commit to working on that single thing intensely for a while.**

- Identify a priority goal or a habit you're trying to acquire.
- Block out a certain number of hours every day to dedicate to it.
- Commit to deep, uninterrupted work towards your goal during this time.
- Keep it up for as long as it takes to reach your goal.

What matters here is not how extreme or punishing your routine is, but rather how intentional you are about it. If you can sustain two full, high-quality hours a day on a goal you care about, then you *will* make progress.

Remember: Choose just one thing at a time. A big part of monk-mode is single-mindedness, whether you're trying to launch a business, write a book, or teach yourself piano.

Block out some daily time and reserve it for quality work. Protect that time like your life depends on it.

- Work offline whenever possible
- Keep your workspace tidy, calm, and quiet

- Use site blockers and time trackers to keep yourself away from online time sinks
- Physically separate yourself from distractions
- Do deep work when you feel most focused (usually 11 a.m., 3 p.m. and 10 p.m.)
- Alert friends, family, and colleagues to your intentions so they don't disturb you

Keep it up!

Monk mode is hard mode. It's not meant to be ultra-easy or accessible without effort.

Don't get discouraged if it takes a long time to build up stamina, focus, and clarity. Those qualities are not free, but are rewards given to those willing to work for them.

However, take heart—every time you shake off a distraction and reaffirm your commitment to work that matters, you are strengthening yourself. You are taking a tiny step towards being a more productive and disciplined person, and simultaneously a step away from being a scattered, ineffectual one.

Track Progress Without Judgment

There is something deeply encouraging about people who consciously choose to live a life according to their values.

Monks overcome the world by *retreating* from it. They may practice a kind of severe asceticism that, although inspirational in an abstract sense, may feel wildly unachievable for everyday people living in the world as we find it.

Monks overcome the world by *retreating* from it.

But we can overcome it while still in it.

The name of the game is **not perfection, but consistency.**

There simply is no point in beating yourself up when you slip off course or fall far below your intentions. In a way, monk-like discipline is not the heroic ability to never fall, but the willingness to fall repeatedly, sometimes multiple times a day, and yet continue to get up again anyway, and keep going.

- **Gently switch your focus**: Instead of dwelling on all the bad that you want to remove from your life, shift your awareness onto all the good that exists already that can be built on and expanded.
- **Stay humble**: The ego wants dramatic, overnight transformation. Instead, be willing to accept modest routines, kept daily. Commitment is a long game, so settle in.
- **Track without judgment**: Getting caught up in shame about your

shortcomings is just another distraction. Be curious, learn from your mistakes, and take active steps to do better next time. You do not learn anything by condemning yourself.

There is no need to punish yourself. There is no intrinsic value in you being miserable. That said, we can always choose to eliminate what is low value in our lives, to focus on what matters and simply refuse to be distracted by what doesn't.

The ability to perform deep work is increasingly rare in our hyperconnected, ultra-online world. That means that it's simultaneously becoming more *valuable*. Cultivating monk-like focus is unfashionable and difficult... but those who can achieve it will thrive.

Chapter 15: Touch It Once Principle

"If you want to make an easy job seem mighty hard, just keep putting off doing it."

- **Richard Miller**

The easiest way to explain the value of the Touch It Once Principle is to show what it *doesn't* look like:

- A simple task lands on your desk—a bill in the mail.
- You look at it and think, "Huh, I need to sort that out at some point."
- You move the bill from one end of the desk to the other, then carry on doing whatever you were doing.
- Some hours later, you remember the task.
- You again think, "Oh yeah, I need to get to that."
- You pick the bill up and file it away in a special place for unpaid bills, then do something else.
- You remember the task again, and this time you're so annoyed you write it on a list of things you've been meaning to get round to—"Pay the damn bill."
- You do something else.
- Several days pass, and you keep transferring this item from yesterday's list to today's. Every transfer, you underline and circle the task more and

more. You take the bill out of the special place, and pin it on the cork board.
- One day it's late at night and you can't sleep. You're thinking about a million things, and one of them is this annoying bill you *still* haven't paid. By this point you've thought about it, made notes about it, and shuffled it around countless times. You've done everything. Except pay it.

The Touch It Once Principle is a close cousin of the Five Minute Rule, i.e., if something takes less than five minutes, just do it as soon as possible and clear it from your mind completely.

Keeping these kinds of "zombie tasks" alive is a unique form of procrastination. The cost is threefold:

- You lose peace of mind because you're mentally carrying a load of unfinished tasks.
- You lose time because you're constantly context switching, multitasking, and dawdling.
- You lose productivity because, well, you're not doing the thing.

Everyone knows that unless you *really* kill zombies the first time round, they just keep coming back. It's the same with zombie tasks.

If you don't do it and do it properly, it has a tendency to keep following you around, taking up way more time, energy, and mental bandwidth than it ever needed to.

The Touch it Once Rule: As soon as you touch something, act on it at once.

Let's open this up a little:

- **"Touch"** – Of course, this applies to everything that comes into our field of awareness, not just things we can literally touch.
- **"Something"** – This can be a demand or request, a task, a piece of mail or a message, a bit of news or an update, a job relating to a project, a chore, or an invitation.
- **"Act"** – This could mean completing the task fully or identifying and planning the next actionable step to take, for example scheduling a time block the following day to tackle it.

Once you cut down on those zombie tasks that won't leave you alone, you remove that stressful residue of "unfinished business" that makes you feel stressed and harangued, and you streamline your workflow right from the moment something new enters your world.

Thinking again about that simple task that landed on your desk, you can imagine that every time you think, "Oh yeah, I have that thing I need to do," you are setting up a tiny speedbump in your thought process and taking away from your focus in the present.

Several days and a ton of stress later, you still haven't done the task... but you've "touched" it a dozen times!

The upgraded version:

- A simple task lands on your desk
- You look at it and think, "Huh, I need to respond to this."
- You respond
- The End

You touch it once, so that you don't have to touch it again.

You can see the irony: In procrastinating certain boring or unenjoyable tasks, we actually amplify them in our world, and draw them out so they last way, way longer.

The Touch It Once Principle is a flowchart disguised as a mindset.

Instead of mentally re-visiting the same tasks over and over and wearing out your mental resources, make an intentional choice just *once*, then move on. Act on a task as soon as you become aware of it, and you'll simply never allow mental clutter to build up and overwhelm you.

Here's exactly how to move through the Touch it Once flowchart:

If the Task Takes Less Than 5 Minutes, Do It Immediately

Small jobs take up more energy to put off than to simply complete. Quickly clear the deck, grab that quick win and move on, enjoying that feeling of instant freedom.

- Don't keep reading and re-reading the same email or letter
- Don't delay signing a document or completing a form
- Don't drag your feet sending a quick message or making an appointment

If it takes less than five minutes, do it the second it hits your inbox or appears in your field of awareness. Prevent re-work. Do it now. If you do it later, you may have to do it again and again and again…

If It Takes More Than 5 Minutes, Decide on the Next Step Now

Remember that "act" in this context also means:

- Make a decision
- Create a plan
- Schedule a future date to do the task

Many tasks fall into this category—you can't do them this very instant, but nevertheless the clock is ticking and you'll have to get around to them sometime.

The best practice is to put something in your calendar right away, or else delegate the task immediately so you can clear it from your mind.

Create a future time block.

Set a reminder on your phone.

Give yourself a due date and break the task into smaller chunks.

(One possibility: Make the decision to ignore the task completely.)

It will only take you a few minutes to process any incoming task this way, and the habit will create a feeling of proactive self-management. After a while it may even start to seem like you just have fewer tasks to do… and in a way, that's true!

If It's Repetitive, Delegate, Automate, or Batch It

The key is to be intentional and to be organized.

Are you noticing that the same *kind* of task keeps cropping up for you again and again? Is it something you are often required to do?

Time to follow the thread even further back along the flowchart:

- Is this a task that can be delegated?
- Is this a task that can be automated?

- Is this a task that can be batched with similar tasks?

If you're routinely bothered by having to pay bills, for example, set up an automated payment to come directly from your account, then set aside some time every month or so to review your bank statements.

Don't keep reinventing the wheel.

Other questions to consider including in the flowchart:

- Does this task even need to be done? (If not, don't do it!)
- Does this task need to be done by me specifically? (If not, consider delegating.)

But isn't this the same as distracted multitasking?

No! When you're in the middle of a work session or time block, mentally agree with yourself that you are not to be disturbed, nor are you going to distract yourself.

Don't randomly check your email or messages.

Don't be available for sudden interruptions or requests.

When you're at the end of a work session or time block, then *intentionally decide* to check your mail. That's the time to apply the Touch It Once Principle.

A great idea is to have a fixed block in your schedule where you specifically tackle emails, messages, and small errands that would otherwise accumulate. For example, get into the habit of checking your email *just once* in the morning at 8 a.m., and then once again at 4 p.m.

If it's not 8 a.m. or 4 p.m.? Then reading or even thinking about emails counts as a distraction.

If it *is* 8 a.m. or 4 p.m., deploy the Touch it Once approach. Tackle incoming tasks on your terms and reclaim your time.

Potential stumbling blocks

It's precisely because the Touch It Once Principle is so simple and obvious that it's easy to forget about it. Particularly if you're an overthinker, have fuzzy boundaries, or your time management habits are out of whack, you may not even see the many ways that you keep "touching" tasks.

Pay attention and notice *when* you're repeatedly returning to tasks, and *why*.

- Do you have a hard time saying no to external demands?
- Are you unclear about what's your responsibility and what isn't?
- Is it sometimes difficult for you to assess how long a task will really take?
- Are you unclear about what your priority is?

- Do you have issues with perfectionism or taking on too much?

The Touch It Once Principle can help shine a light on places in your schedule where time, energy, and focus are leaking. However, it cannot always tell you *why* it's happening. You may need to do a little extra investigative work if the same patterns keep cropping up for you.

Examples:

You keep being interrupted by colleagues who ask, "Have you got a minute?" and then proceed to drop hours of work in your lap. The issue here is either weak boundaries and poorly defined roles, or people-pleasing.

You waste time responding to every random Facebook wall post and then returning to follow the threads. The issue here is that the task doesn't really need to be done in the first place.

You keep receiving update emails and being bcc-ed into various threads. Each time, you stop what you're doing to read through all these messages that don't strictly concern you. The issue here is a lack of clarity on your focus, priority, and goals, and perhaps confusion about what is and isn't expected of you.

Even better than Touch it Once? Identifying those things you *don't have to touch at all:*

- You don't have to attend every meeting.

- You don't have to respond to every notification.
- You don't have to react to every change or update.

From the top, then, the flowchart looks a little something like this:

1. **Does this stimulus really require my attention or reaction?** (if not, ignore)
2. **Does this task need to be done?** (if not, ignore)
3. **Does this task need to be done by *me*?** (if no, ignore or delegate)
4. **Will this task take me less than 5 minutes?** (if no, decide on next steps now, if yes, do it immediately)
5. **Does this task keep on appearing?** (if yes, consider delegating, automating, or batching to streamline)

Keep telling yourself that distractions, bids for your attention, interruptions, and requests are *not automatically entitled to your time or energy*. By running through this flowchart, you reclaim your right to sort through incoming demands in a rational way that works for you.

We'll be expanding on this flow in a later chapter.

Chapter 16: Self-Competition

"I am in competition with no one. I run my own race. I have no desire to play the game of being better than anyone, in any way, shape, or form. I just aim to improve, to be better than I was before. That's me and I'm free."

- **Jenny Perry**

Here's a deep question: Why be productive in the first place?

What is, ultimately, the driver for personal growth, improvement, and the setting and achieving goals?

People run races against one another, they go to battle, they pit their strength and intellect and stamina against their peers, and they willingly rank and judge their worth relative to their rivals. Whether it's in politics, business, sports, or life in general, achievement and productivity have always been strongly connected with the competitive impulse.

After all, when people say they want to reach "the top", what are they actually saying? They want to be on top of a pile made of people who have performed and produced to a lesser extent than themselves.

Competition can be a powerful motivator... Right?

Maybe not quite.

A fascinating study by Merryman and Bronson tested the attitudes of Princeton University students (*Top Dog: The Science of Winning and Losing*, Ebury Press, 2014). They were sorted into two groups:

Group 1 was asked to say which high school they'd gone to, in a way that strongly insinuated that they didn't quite deserve their place at the prestigious university and had been lucky to get in at all. They were also given an "Intellectual Ability Questionnaire" purposely designed to be intimidating, again with the suggestion that if they did poorly, it would reveal a lack of deserving to be at Princeton.

Group 2 were also asked about their high school but after they took the same test, which had a much less intimidating title: "Intellectual Challenge Questionnaire".

Interestingly, the two groups performed very differently on the intellectual tests.

Group 1: 72% correct answers

Group 2: 90% correct answers

The authors claim that "In a competitive situation our bodies can experience the same level of stress hormones as jumping out of a plane."

But competition may not be the problem. Rather, fear-based strategies as a whole can induce stress that undermines performance.

Competition may make you feel "motivated" to do more, but could actually hinder your output in the long run.

Wanting to outperform others is not true motivation. It's a survival reaction.

FOMO, insecurity, and jealousy are simply not the same as real drive and ambition.

When you compete against others you:

- Are subject to external rules and standards, meaning you don't proactively establish your own.
- Increase your sense of threat and lack, which creates stress and feelings of inadequacy that may linger even after you've "won".
- You are playing someone else's game, which disempowers you.

A little friendly friction now and then can certainly get you to up your game, but this kind of competitiveness is not sustainable.

It will never be a substitute for a genuine, mature, and internal locus of control, i.e., "I control my own destiny, I make my own meaning, and I govern myself—regardless of how I compare to others."

No need to follow others.

No need to bring others down.

No need for them and their achievements to be involved at all.

When you compete again yourself, you:

- Take responsibility for identifying your own values, goals, and standards.
- Operate from curiosity, excitement, and sincere hunger for growth and development, instead of just fear.
- Are free to set goals that align with your values and vision.

Essentially, ranking yourself against an earlier version of yourself is about harnessing the power of competition but without the fear, lack, or insecurity.

It's about self-authorship.

It's about conscious, meaningful action that flows from within.

It's about holding yourself accountable to yourself.

When we compete with ourselves, there isn't a loser. There is only your future self to continuously look up to.

Comparison, as they say, is the thief of joy. Let's add to that: Competitiveness is the killer of *genuine* ambition.

Beat Yesterday's Effort, Not Someone Else's Outcome

One day, you're going along, minding your own business. You start scrolling and social media hopping, and within a few minutes, that familiar old sensation creeps in: Oh man, *I'm falling behind in life.*

The comparison-competition loop is activated, and you suddenly feel compelled to act, to achieve, to perform, to produce.

"Maybe I should be doing more."

"Maybe I should be working faster."

But that feeling you're experiencing? That compulsion to strive and achieve and prove yourself? It's not real. It's not a genuine desire for growth.

It's just fear.

The ironic thing is that when you are in this state of mind, you are actually pulled further away from what sincerely matters to you. Away from your passion. Your values, your innate talents.

Maybe your focus subtly shifts from *being* better to *looking* better—you may start to wonder less about achieving your goals and more about the external markers of those goals, and how you might be validated for them (or shamed if you don't have them!).

Let's try to reframe: You are not interested in the *superficial performance* of success. You are not competing. You will not be ranked and rated relative to others.

Instead, **you are competing against the only other person who matters here—your past self.**

Don't be reactive.

Don't be a slave to fear.

Let go of performance.

Let go of appearances.

When you compete against others, you're defending, proving, reacting, asking others for permission, and granting them the ability to authenticate your worth.

When you compete against yourself, you're growing, developing, and improving.

You're no longer chasing "the competition" or running away from failure. You're unfolding.

The thing is that this mindset shift is the one most reliably associated with high performers, and the kind of people others want to emulate.

Driven from within, you'll be more focused, more motivated, more resilient, more authentic, and more creative.

You won't burn out as easily because the fuel in your tank is not fear, shame, or inadequacy.

Keep it simple: What did you do yesterday? See if you can do a little more today.

That's it! No need to waste time considering where other people are and what they're doing.

- If you worked on your essay yesterday for 15 minutes, aim for 20 minutes today.
- If you hit 10 quality reps of a certain exercise at gym during your last workout, aim for 11 at your next workout.
- If you made $100 on a new side hustle last week, aim to make $120 this week.

Don't copy others. Don't concern yourself with their routes through life, or the pace at which they're moving. Instead, find the joy in becoming your own yardstick.

Progress is personal. Teach yourself what you're capable of—reaching your own milestones will always be sweeter than following along after someone else's.

Track Metrics That Reflect Your Values, Not Your Ego

Have you ever met someone who is by all accounts successful and accomplished, yet they're still deeply unhappy and unfulfilled?

They've ticked all the boxes. But it then turns out that those boxes were never all that important to them in the first place, and so their achievements never created any real feelings of satisfaction.

It can be all too easy for other people's ambitions to quietly creep in and replace our own. We may see someone else achieving a certain income level, lifestyle, or possession, for example, and automatically assume that that bar is something we ourselves desire.

But is that just vanity talking?

What is *your* true north?

What are *your* values?

Who are *you* deep down, and who do you want to become in this one special life that you will never get a second chance at?

Prioritize becoming over winning.

When you can comfortably rest in your own unconditional sense of self-worth, then you do not see the accomplishment of goals as a kind of remedy—i.e., something you're compelled to do to make up for the fact that you're insecure about who you actually are.

Instead, you can lean into who you actually are and allow your actions to stem from your authentic values and principles.

Are you really satisfied with the world's picture of what a successful person looks like? Or could you expand that definition? Make it richer? More meaningful? More *you*?

Let's put this in practical terms:

- In a broad sense, who are you trying to be? (Note: not do, but *be*).
- Pick 1-3 habits that align with this vision of yourself (Note: not single outcomes but lifelong habits).
- Get to work cementing these habits into your daily life, then measure your consistency with these, rather than measuring yourself against other people's metrics.

There are lots of ideas out there about the habits associated with wealth and success, but unless they actively help you become the person you want to be, you don't have to adopt them.

Examples:

- Instead of trying to reach some arbitrary number of hours worked per week, track

how many days in a row you can commit to a solid session of deep work.
- Instead of obsessing over follower counts, keep track of how often you're hitting "publish" and how happy *you* are with what you're putting out there.
- Instead of pushing yourself to acquire a brag-worthy physique, track your health and wellbeing, and measure your overall sense of peace, flow, and purpose.

When you reorient your awareness to internal wins, not only do you reduce stress and feelings of inferiority, but you also cultivate real motivation for yourself. Why? Because you're focusing on what matters, and you're focusing on what's actually under your control.

Run a Weekly "Self-review"

If you're driven by competition and the desire to live up to external standards, you're constantly measuring yourself against someone who isn't you.

Someone who doesn't have your limitations or strengths, someone who hasn't had your history, and someone who doesn't share your vision. Basically, you're always referencing yourself against someone else—and that someone else is not you.

Instead, **focus on self-referencing**, i.e., comparing your current self to your past and to your future self.

At the end of every week or month, take a moment to check in:

- What version of me showed up this week/month?
- What helped me move forward?
- What got in my way?
- What's missing/what do I need?

By asking these questions, you can make adjustments to your overall strategy. Over time, you grow and improve.

If, however, your only measure of success is external, you end up asking all the wrong questions: What do other people think of me? What will they say about XYZ?

The trouble is that what works for them might not be right for you. The only way to find out what *is* right for you is to test it out in your own life.

Comparison is about perfection. About finally reaching some ideal state and then just... stopping.

Self-competition is not about perfection, but iteration. You never stop becoming the person you are.

Competition: Present-you is and always will be less-than. No learning. Just eternal inadequacy and playing catch-up.

Self-competition: Future-you benefits because present-you learns from past-you. And keeps on learning!

Self-review doesn't have to be prolonged or ultra-serious; it can be as simple as noticing that you're skipping more workouts than usual, and trying out to find out why. It can look like noticing what you're doing well and challenging yourself to find ways to do more of it. It can even be zooming in on failures and mistakes, mining the experience for insight, and deliberately setting yourself a new goal to do just 10% better next time.

Be good today. Be better tomorrow. That's enough work to focus on; there's no need to concern yourself with anybody else!

Chapter 17: Productive Cognitive Load

"Just as a man working with his tools should know its limitations, a man working with his cognitive apparatus must know its limitations."

- Charlie Munger

Have you ever been browsing the internet or using your phone when things start to slow down or freeze completely?

You have too many open tabs, the page you're loading is riddled with ads and videos, or you have too many energy-guzzling apps open. Your device has reached its processing limits.

The same thing can happen with your brain, which also has finite processing capacity.

The theory of cognitive load and its terminology was first put forward by psychologist John Sweller.

Cognitive load: The amount of work we're giving our brains to do at any one time. Some examples: remembering a phone number, following a map, learning a foreign language, unpacking a complex scientific concept, or solving a problem.

Cognitive overload: The work outstrips your brain's capacity, and you feel overwhelmed.

You'll know that you've veered into cognitive overload when you crash and freeze just like a computer does. You may "go blank" or feel completely stressed and dazed.

Sweller made a further distinction:

Intrinsic cognitive load: The size, weight, and difficulty inherent in the task itself, as well as our pre-existing abilities, knowledge, and aptitudes.

Extrinsic cognitive load: Influenced by how the task is presented, for example the distractions that come along with it, the study materials used to explain it, or the environment it takes place in.

Cognitive overload happens when extrinsic + intrinsic load equals an amount that outstrips our capacity. When we're in this state, it's no surprise that:

- our attention fractures
- our comprehension goes out the window
- our productivity plummets
- we lose speed and accuracy
- our motivation slackens
- we remember less
- we make more mistakes
- our decision-making suffers
- we lose resilience
- our creativity takes a hit

- oh, and the cherry on top is exhaustion and burn out!

The idea of cognitive load makes intuitive sense, but many of us fail to really grasp our own cognitive limits, let alone respect them.

We believe that we think merely with our "minds" without considering that our *brains* are physical organs, which can tire just like any other part of our body.

Information is infinite. Our mental resources are not.

If you're having trouble being productive, disciplined, or focused, one reason you may not have considered is this: You're cognitively overloaded.

The emails, the scrolling, the news sites, the multitasking, the distractions, the notifications, the interruptions, the endless errands… these things don't have to be especially difficult or challenging to take up cognitive bandwidth.

Another way to say this is: Sometimes a lack of productivity is not about intelligence, motivation, knowledge, or willpower. It's about the simple fact that you've blown your capacity.

If this sounds like you, then the solution is not to increase intelligence, willpower, motivation, etc. The solution is to *strategically manage and reduce cognitive load* wherever possible.

If you're in cognitive overload, your higher order executive functions will suffer, no matter how sophisticated your organization tools, or how sincere your commitment to the cause.

Important: Your brain is *built* to work and process information. Managing cognitive load doesn't mean avoiding effort. It simply means acknowledging that the brain works best within a defined, moderate range. Our goal is to respect our limits and optimize, so that we're always using what we have wisely, and making space for the efforts that matter most.

Enter one more distinction:

Germane load: The productive effort that helps you better understand, connect, learn, or remember. In other words, this productive load is the effort you make to reduce overall effort.

Our goal?

- Manage intrinsic load
- Minimize extrinsic load
- Maximize germane load

Let's take a closer look at how to do that.

Get Another Brain to Manage High Intrinsic Load

Recall that intrinsic load is the size, weight, and difficulty inherent in the task itself, as well as our pre-existing abilities, knowledge, and aptitudes.

Some tasks are intellectually demanding because that's their nature. Here are some things that have high intrinsic load:

- Planning a complicated, multi-person, multi-country holiday with several intersecting parameters and constraints, under a time limit
- Navigating your way through some obscure and vaguely threatening tax laws that you can't make head nor tail of
- Understanding difficult concepts like game theory, fluid dynamics, renormalization, or bond convexity

However, a task doesn't have to be academic or even especially "difficult" to drain you. After all, a very basic appliance can nevertheless draw a lot of electricity.

Until humans invent an IQ boosting pill, **a good rule of thumb for managing high intrinsic load is to seek out back up:**

- Ask for help, advice, or just someone to talk through the problem with you
- Break things down and take one step at a time, or get a pro or mentor to tackle the trickier parts for you
- Consider using AI tools, but be extremely careful—if you're in the dark about a

topic, you won't necessarily be able to spot misinformation or misdirection

If a task feels too overwhelming, break it down, take it slow, and use whatever tricks you can to simplify. Collaborate or delegate. What part of the load can you shrug off? Identify the most important or most impactful aspect, then trim away the rest for now.

Use Mind Mapping to Reduce Extraneous Load

Recall that extrinsic load is the burden contained in how the task is presented; for example:

- The format the information takes, e.g. visual, auditory, presented all at once, presented linearly, and so on
- The style and layout of study materials
- The environment in which you need to do the task
- Time limits and other pressures
- Distractions and interruptions
- Your mood and approach to the task

To simplify, extrinsic load comes down to:

1. Task format
2. Task environment

Here, we'll be focusing primarily on the first kind, having already explored ways to reduce distractions and create a workspace conducive to deep work.

Every task comes with an additional cognitive burden that is over and above the actual mental cost of doing the task. For example, understanding fluid dynamics is a heavy load, but in addition to grasping the concept, your brain has to process all the written information, diagrams, and spoken presentations. Your brain also spends effort to tune out distractions during study sessions, and to self-regulate emotionally (very hard to do with something as frustrating as fluid dynamics!).

The rule of thumb here is to **cut down on noise, clutter, and irrelevancy, and find clarity.**

- Don't repeat yourself (DRY), reduce rework, and apply the Touch It Once Principle
- Cut down on distractions and time craters, which are very cognitively heavy
- Create a SSOT (single source of truth) and allow the organization inherent in it to do the thinking, so you don't have to hold it all in your head
- Schedule cognitively demanding tasks for times when you're available and maximally alert
- Take distraction-evading measures

Our goal should be to bring extrinsic cognitive load as close to zero as possible.

One great way to reduce extrinsic load is to play around with the format of the information we take in. Mind maps are a surprisingly good tool, not just for brainstorming and organization, but for reducing cognitive load and bringing calm and clarity.

A mind map makes information easier to navigate, so you spend less effort muddling through it. Incidentally, making a mind map *is* effort, but it represents germane load—the kind of effort that pays off by making your overall process simpler.

Here's a neat definition from the University of Adelaide Writing Centre:

> *"Mind mapping is an effective means to take notes and brainstorm essay topics. A mind map involves writing down a central theme and thinking of new and related ideas which radiate out from the centre. By focusing on key ideas written down in your own words and looking for connections between them, you can map knowledge in a way that will help you to better understand and retain information."*

You can use mind maps in many different ways:

- To stimulate creativity and generate new ideas
- To visually map out existing ideas and clearly visualize hierarchical

relationships, causal links, connections, and associations
- Logically organize material into categories and subcategories
- Help you work your way through a problem or decision
- Gather information in one place so you can revise and review for text preparation

You may have created "mindless mind maps" in school, but many of us have never learned to use this method to its fullest advantage.

Remember: The mere act of creating a mind map doesn't magically grant you deeper comprehension or memory. Rather, the value of the mind map lies in *how well its structure encodes information.*

How can we use mind maps, and their structure, to reduce extrinsic cognitive load?

The idea is to **depict the same information in a format that is less cognitively demanding (read: *easier*).**

Step 1: Start by writing the main theme/idea/question/topic in the center of the page

Step 2: Gradually add branches to illustrate concepts that connect to the central theme

Step 3: Use color, position on the page, sizing, different kinds of lines, shapes, and other symbols to represent relationships

Making mind maps takes time and effort, but constantly check that this is germane load, not just more extrinsic load. How can you tell the difference? Keep asking yourself: *Is what I'm doing making anything easier, simpler, or clearer?* If so, then it's germane. If not, you may just be giving yourself more to think about.

A few tips:

- Don't take notes, then later convert them to mind maps. Instead, cut out the additional step and create mind maps from the start. Your goal is to reduce the number of things you have to do, not increase it
- Don't overload your mind map. Identify key themes and express them in short phrases or headings. You're creating a frame, not duplicating every single fact you know
- It doesn't have to be pretty—just logical. There's no need to spend a lot of time creating a perfect work of art
- Be consistent. You can use any symbols you like, but then continue with that convention, or else you risk increasing cognitive load again

Use Chunking to Increase Germane Load and Memory

Chunking: A magic trick where you reduce the size of what your brain has to store and process, without reducing the size of the information itself.

It's minimizing cognitive load with *no information loss.*

If you treat 10 ideas as 10 separate entities, then you have 10 items to remember and keep track of.

If you chunk those 10 items into separate groups, then you may only have 3 or 4 distinct items to manage.

Chunking is a way to use *structured organization* and natural associations between ideas to do some of the brain work for you. **The more structure, the lower the load, and the more you can process.**

Examples:

- Instead of memorizing a list of twenty items on a shopping list, you can group them into four main chunks: green things, soup ingredients, things beginning with P, things that go in the top shelf of the cupboard, etc.
- Instead of wading through a complicated literary essay or philosophical argument,

you can break things down: introduction, three main arguments, two sub arguments, conclusion.
- Instead of trying to memorize an entire mathematical formula or chemical reaction, break it down into smaller pieces, then tell yourself a story about each section, drilling those first, then connecting everything together again.

Alternative Tips (If You Didn't Like the Previous Ones)

A cognitive load reduction strategy only works if... it works. If for whatever reason the above tips and techniques don't hit the spot, try the following:

Remind yourself of what you already know – Before starting a new task, recall and write down your existing knowledge. This reduces intrinsic load, making the task feel cognitively and psychologically smaller. The task may still be hard, but you're not starting from zero, and you can get to the point faster.

Keep cutting to the chase – Always be simplifying, streamlining, and trimming away clutter. Trying to figure out what's going on is extraneous load. Reduce it by simplifying instructions, clearing space, getting organized, and breaking things down, so you're always working on just one task at a time.

When your brain says it's done, listen – Are you feeling stuck, depleted, or frazzled? That's your brain telling you it's overloaded. You gain nothing by forcing yourself to do more (hint: you can't). Step back, take a break. Catch your breath and then look carefully to see where most of the load is coming from, then adjust. Sometimes, all you need is a moment to restore and refresh before re-engaging.

Protect and declutter your workspace – Staying tidy and organized increases germane load. Have your tools and materials close at hand and well-organized, create a supportive SSOT, declutter regularly, and maintain a distraction-free environment that is ergonomic and comfortable.

Keep checking in with priorities – Carry only the highest-impact and most important tasks and shake off the rest. Multitasking is a one-way ticket to stress and overwhelm.

Use technology, but wisely – Tools and apps can relieve distraction, or they can be the source of the distraction. Don't find a way to retrofit a digital tool onto your life. Instead, ask what support you need then seek out a tool that fits the description.

Practice self-care – You already know the drill. Your brain is a part of your body, which means that it works better when supported with adequate sleep, nutrition, and exercise.

Chapter 18: Work Backwards
"Begin with the end in mind."

- **Stephen Covey**

Working backwards is exactly what it sounds like: **We begin with the endpoint we're aiming for, and then in light of that, we consider each of the steps required to land there.** Step by step, we work in reverse order, planning out each stage of the journey.

It's a perspective shift that makes a lot of sense. When you work forwards, you're taking for granted that you know exactly where you're going, and exactly the route to take to get there. But sometimes… you don't.

What's more, it's easy to get sidetracked or waste time on things that don't matter when you're essentially making things up as you go along.

By beginning at the end, though, you're setting a clearly defined outcome as your focus. This outcome acts like a magnet, so that all your actions and efforts along the way are pulled in the same direction.

You're more productive because you're more focused.

Your efforts are more defined, so they're more impactful.

You aren't just working hard; your efforts have direction.

If you have a goal, the working backwards approach can help you bring more power, focus, and strategy to what you're doing.

- You'll be forced to find clarity and precision in how you see the goal
- You'll outline a realistic trajectory for how to get there
- You'll gather momentum and start banking small, everyday wins
- You'll look ahead and empower yourself to plan for contingencies and possible setbacks
- You'll bring more structure and clarity to your workflow—which means less stress and fluster
- When you know *what* you're doing, you actually give yourself more flexibility in *how* you do it, so you can innovate and problem-solve better

That said, working backwards is less appropriate for very simple or short-term goals, or situations where habits, processes, and adaptive strategies in the moment are more important than fixed outcomes.

Flip the script

Productivity suffers when we are reactive and wasting our time putting out little fires while the bigger, more important tasks go unfinished.

Change your perspective: Your priority is not what seems most urgent or front of mind right now (honestly? That's code for "distraction"). Your priority is always the next step on your plan. That step that you need to take today to get to where you want to be tomorrow.

Step 1: Start at the Finish Line

An uncomfortable truth: Many of us have no idea what we're working towards.

We may have some vague, second-hand idea of our goal, but when it comes down to it, our lack of imagination means we haven't truly fleshed out this vision. It's very much a hypothetical thing that belongs to the mists of an unknown future.

Time to change that!

Your destination needs to be super, ultra, crystal clear.

Imprecise goals often conceal faulty assumptions or unrealistic expectations. Don't just set a default goal and assume that the details will sort themselves out—either you'll fail to get there or you'll get there and realize that "there" isn't quite what you wanted after all.

The more clearly you can visualize the end, the easier it will be to reverse-engineer your path to it.

Vague goals are like daydreams. They have less substance than clouds. A fuzzy vision leads to lukewarm action which leads to... well, nothing usually.

Start at the end.

- What does the world actually look like once you've achieved this goal?
- What are you doing, saying, thinking, and feeling?
- What is different about your environment—be specific and concrete.
- In what ways are *you* different?

Whether your goal is big or small, it needs to be clear in your mind for two reasons: **You need to believe in the vision—both that it's logically but also emotionally possible**. Only then can your brain get to work finding the route to get there.

For example, instead of setting the goal, "study biology," define it as "complete and quiz myself on flashcards for Chapters 3–6 by Thursday night."

Instead of saying "improve violin," say "feel confident playing a full Grade 4 violin piece by the end of March."

Step 2: Identify Milestones in Reverse

Now work backwards: What comes immediately *before* you achieve the final goal?

Identify that last step in the marathon just before you cross the finish line. This is a checkpoint. Now, what happens before that? And before *that*?

In this way you gradually work backwards, locating checkpoints and milestones until you come to the present. This process may seem simple, but it can be extremely valuable:

- It reveals clear, actionable steps, which are often less intimidating than you first thought
- It gives you an idea of order and process, so that a structured program/schedule starts to come together
- It gives you a sense of purpose and direction, while also reducing overwhelm and pressure—you know you don't have to do everything at once

Let's consider this process using our violin example. Let's say that it's January 4th now, and we need to work backwards from the end of March.

- The last week of March: Full drills of complete piece
- The first three weeks of March: Practice final third of the piece

- February: Practice second third of the piece
- Rest of January: Practice first third of the piece
- First week of January: Review piece, practice required scales and fingering

As you're putting these milestones together, you might wonder how much detail is too much detail. Generally, you want to start by identifying the biggest milestones and creating a broad framework first.

It's up to you how much you want to break things down, but a good rule of thumb is that the bigger or more complex the goal, the more milestones you'll need. Try to avoid overanalyzing; you'll need to retain a little wiggle room for spontaneous adjustments along the way.

Remember: For now you're just identifying milestones, not explaining how you'll reach them.

Step 3: Build a Reverse Timeline With Real Deadlines

Every mini goal generates a new dopamine hit for you, and this rewards your forward momentum and keeps you feeling on track and motivated. For the process to work, though, you need to actually hit these targets on a realistic timeline.

Carefully plug all the checkpoints above into your calendar, in reverse order. Now they are deadlines.

Where possible, anchor them to pre-existing time blocks, and allocate realistic and specific periods where you will work on the relevant task. You're planning, but you're simultaneously holding yourself accountable—these are no longer hopes and wishes, but commitments.

You're making a date with yourself, so act today in a manner that means you'll be showing up to that appointment promptly!

In our example, this stage may look like blocking out a daily hour session for violin practice, or possibly expanding an existing practice session. This step may take a little time, but again, it's germane cognitive load. It's work you do now to avoid decision fatigue and overwhelm later.

Take a deep breath. Thank yourself for being proactive. You are no longer on the hook for a massive project. **All you have to focus on now is the small assigned task in front of you**. Just keep focusing on that next bite-sized chunk task. If you do, you *will* get where you need to go.

How reassuring is that?

Troubleshooting

Don't be surprised when things don't go to plan. Just because you encounter a few hiccups and setbacks doesn't mean that the plan is invalid or that you need to give up.

Any route that carries you from where you are now to the place you want to be in the future will require a degree of *fine-tuning, adjustment, and iteration.*

You've laid the framework in place, but the day-to-day work is all about discovering ways to meet those milestones. At the end of every week or month, ask yourself:

- What have I learned?
- What worked well and how can I do more of it?
- What didn't work and what can I do instead?

Changing the plans as you go along isn't a sign of failure. It's proof that you can be adaptable and responsive.

Instead of focusing on, "I can't do this right" or "I didn't reach this milestone" shift focus: What *did* you do right? If your first plan doesn't work, become curious: What *would* work? Try that.

With your vision firmly in place, you can experiment with confidence to find alternate routes to reach your destination.

Being rigid? That only maximizes the possible ways for you to "fail".

Stay alert to new opportunities and chances to do things even better than you originally planned. Be prepared to collaborate, receive feedback, or go faster than you anticipated.

You don't have to have the entire plan plotted out in painful detail; but with a solid framework in place, you can strike a balance between accountability and flexibility.

Always remember: A goal without a plan is just a wish.

And a goal, no matter how grand and ambitious, *is* achievable… so long as you have a plan.

Chapter 19: Clean Slate Method

"The real voyage of discovery consists not in seeking new landscapes, but in having new eyes."

- **Marcel Proust**

Have you ever been slogging away at a problem for hours, only to have someone walk by and instantly spot the solution, without even trying?

Their "fresh eyes" were able to see what your tired, bogged down eyes couldn't.

This is a counterintuitive but very real phenomenon. **Sometimes, the more we stare at a particular task, the less of it we can see.**

We're just too close.

It's like we get stuck in tunnel vision, lose that initial zing, and find ourselves stumped or quickly running out of steam.

- You keep reading and rereading the same sentence
- You're repeating yourself or going in circles
- You're feeling distracted, numb, bored

Your eyes are no longer fresh.

Have you ever tried saying a particular word over and over again until it starts to seem really weird to you? If not, try it now: Say "milk" over and over again and see how quickly it starts to lose meaning and break down into mere sound.

The same thing happens with tasks, and not just creative ones.

It's not that you're lazy, distracted, or struggling with something too difficult. It's not even a question of cognitive overload. It's just that sometimes, we can get too close to a thing.

Solution: We need distance.

The Clean Slate Method reminds us that good work isn't always a question of *more* work—sometimes it's about looking away long enough to refresh our eyes, so to speak. It comes to us from the author of *The Creative Act*, Rick Rubin (2023).

Clean the slate, shake that Etch-a-Sketch board, and start over. You'll return to the task with:

- Better judgment
- More creativity
- Smarter decision-making
- Quicker work
- The ability to spot solutions

Let's look at exactly how:

Set a 24-Hour Cooldown Before Reviewing a Task

If you're working on an important project, you may find yourself tempted to keep going… and going. You keep returning to it to double check this detail, add something here, remove something there.

You're not letting the project *breathe*… and your perspective suffers.

When you're done with a project—or even a part of a project—give it a rest, literally. **Let things settle and let your brain reset for at least a full day, longer, if possible.**

Don't look at it. Don't even think about it.

Just forget about it for a while and allow yourself to disentangle from the work. You could even literally seal the project away in a locked drawer or closed envelope with strict instructions: ONLY TO BE OPENED ON TUESDAY 5th, 9 a.m.

When you return, your perception will be far more neutral. You'll be able to clearly spot errors and weak points, and you'll have a far more accurate view of what's working well.

If you're too close, on the other hand, your assessment may be pretty biased—in either direction!

Stay fresh. As far as possible, build in spaces and off-days between your work sessions. When you sit down to do the task again, pause for a second. Close your eyes and take a deep breath. Forget everything that's come before and just be here, now.

Deliberately tell yourself,

"I am encountering this task for the very first time."

Put on a stranger's eyes and look with a gaze ready to see what's new and interesting, instead of what's already known, imperfect, or calcified.

Tip: Of course, you can actually enlist the help of real strangers and their eyes. For example, hire beta readers, test users, or others who can give you feedback and opinions on your work. Just choose them wisely, get a range of opinions, and find an average, and make a habit of never asking the same people twice in a row.

View Your Work in a Different Format

Let's say you're working on a report or essay. There are several spelling and grammatical errors that have been missed by spellcheck, but *you've* also missed them. Why? Because as your tired mind runs over those sentences again and again, it takes little cognitive shortcuts and helpfully "fills in the gaps" with what it assumes is there, or should be.

Those little errors become all but invisible to you.

However, if you suddenly change the layout of the task, and your brain is no longer blurring out those errors for you, everything will suddenly present itself more clearly to your awareness.

Even small changes can kick your brain out of its tendency to skim over things on autopilot:

- Try a different font or font size, or change the size of the text on the screen
- Switch from landscape to portrait orientation or vice versa
- Look at things on your phone or iPad instead of your desktop computer
- Have somebody read the words aloud to you, or simply take the time to read your own work aloud, instead of quietly in your head (this is extremely useful!)
- Print documents so you are reading off of hard copies and not screens
- Toggle a spreadsheet's layout, change the format of dates, or reverse the axes of graphs
- If your work is visual, invert its colors or flip its orientation. Look at it in a mirror or upside down, or view it under different kinds of lighting
- If you're creating music, record yourself with different tools and play the recording back in a range of different ways—earphones, in the car, using quality speakers, etc.

Not only will a quick format change shine a spotlight on awkward phrases, errors, or missing information, but it will also help you to be a better judge of overall quality and flow, whatever the nature of your project.

This is because your brain will be seeing things as though they were new.

You trade in creative blindness for a new perspective.

Change Locations Before You Make Important Edits or Decisions

Sometimes the only way to "see things differently" is to *literally* change the way you're looking. Change your posture or position. Physically get up and move.

Our viewpoints and thought processes are always linked to the environments in which they emerged. That means that **a change in environment can lead to a change in perspective.**

Sometimes, the rigidity and stagnation we experience around an idea is really just a reflection of the narrowness of our approach; i.e., we have been sitting in the same chair, day after day, facing the same direction, staring at the same limited set of symbols, with our bodies held in the same posture.

Our minds are running along the same old ruts, in the same old way, on the same old timeline.

When you think of it like this, it's amazing that we ever have creative ideas at all!

- Do you have to make a big decision?

- Are you facing a particularly knotted problem?
- Are you considering making significant changes to your work?

If so, it's worth first changing your location in space or time to see if you can shake up any stale thinking. This will give you enhanced insight into a problem, it will bring more clarity about a potential decision, and show flaws and strengths in a new light.

- Don't make edits to a document in the same seat you first wrote it in
- Read and re-read proposals, reports, and important emails in different rooms of your house, and at different times of day
- Vary your posture: Stand if you've been sitting, face a different direction, sit in a different chair or on the floor, or even lie flat on your back as you mull over big questions
- If possible, do your work outside or even while walking. Being immersed in natural rather than man-made environments typically brings a whole new perspective
- Reconsider things in the morning if you usually work on them at night, or vice versa. Change your internal environment by revisiting ideas when you're hungry/not hungry, or vary how caffeinated you are!

Here's an example. You may see an end-of-the-world type email on your harsh phone screen at 10 p.m. on a Monday night in your cluttered home office, and immediately respond in a certain way. Yet that email looks far less intimidating when revisited in the light of day, once you've had breakfast, and you read those same words out loud.

In the same way, a business idea that seemed ultra-promising when you first brainstormed it while on holiday in the summer may seem a little less bulletproof when you're travelling home again on a cramped plane, nursing a hangover.

It's not that changing the task format or your own position in space/time allows you to see the "truth"—it's just that the more viewpoints you have on an idea, the less narrow, limited, or rigid your perspective will be.

Don't rush. Don't assume that your old ways of doing things are necessarily the best.

Keep reminding yourself to pause, cleanse your palate, and look at things anew. **Your brain has processing limits**; there is only so much work it can do at once.

But **it also has perception limits**—there is only so much of an idea it can perceive at any one time.

Your perspective is like the narrow beam of a flashlight shining on some unknown object in the dark. Things may be perfectly bright and clear within that small circle of light, but unless you move the beam around, you are not going to get a full picture of the unknown object.

Stay limber, stay fresh.

Don't let your perspective get stuck for too long in any one place.

Chapter 20: Focus Funnel

"Be disciplined about what you respond and react to. Not everyone or everything deserves your time energy and attention."

- **Lalah Delia**

Throughout this book so far, we've explored many different productivity tips, methods, approaches, and tools.

You've probably noticed some significant overlap (e.g. Time Pockets and the principles of NET), while some act almost as counterbalances to one another (going all out in Monk Mode versus dialing back effort to reduce Cognitive Load).

It's as though we have a big toolbox full of different tools.

Now what?

The most important thing—and the step that many productivity gurus fail to address—is finding a logical, intentional, and effective way to *bring all these tools together.*

After all, a tool that just sits there is not really a tool at all. It only derives its value and purpose when we consciously put it to use—and for that we need to know:

- What we're doing with it
- Why

- When
- To what end

In this final chapter, we're going to try and put all our tools together, but in a way that really makes sense for our lives and our goals. We're going to consider how to combine methods and approaches into a single funnel which we'll call the Focus Funnel.

Originally created by Rory Vaden, this method acts like a kind of filter or flowchart. It also helps you appraise and incorporate new strategies as you encounter them.

We pass every new task and incoming demand through the Focus filter, which is structured loosely as follows:

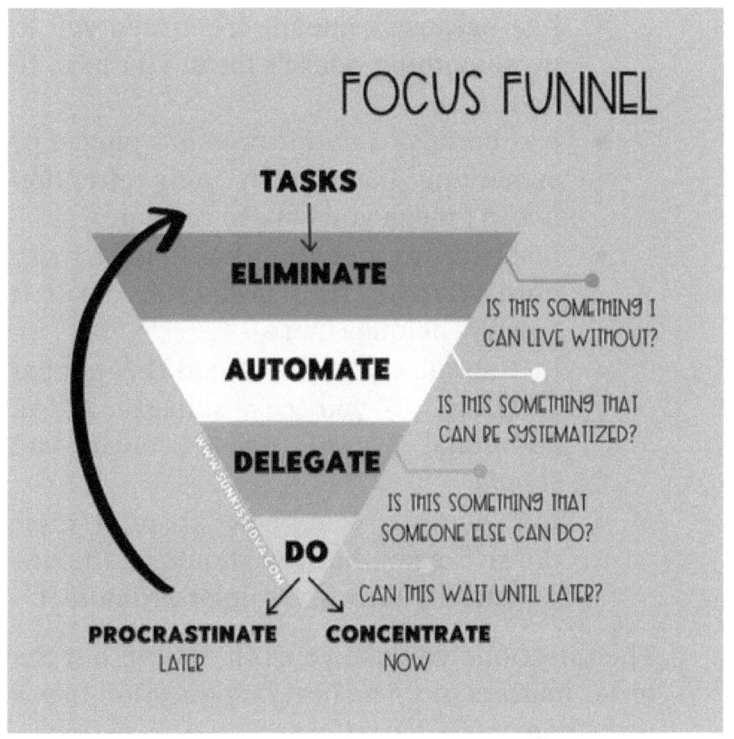

You'll recognize many of the steps already, as they form the core of the approaches we've explored so far: automation, delegation, scheduling later, concentration… this funnel is essentially the Buyback Loop idea (recall Chapter 7) in the form of a process.

Take a look at the very top of the funnel: We ask ourselves the question, **"Does this task actually need to be done at all?"**

- Just because someone has asked you to do something doesn't mean you have to do it.
- Just because a notification has pinged or something has caught your attention doesn't mean you have to respond.
- Just because something has found its way onto your To Do list doesn't mean it actually belongs there.
- Just because you *can* attend this or that meeting, or you *can* squeeze in an additional errand, doesn't mean you *should*.
- Just because you know about a topic doesn't mean that you should be the one to teach it, write about it, or promote it.

The questions you ask yourself matter, but the order matters too: The best *first* question to ask is the one above. Variations:

- Is this relevant?
- Can I live without this?
- Is this a task worth doing?
- Does this require a reaction from me at all?

There's simply no point trying to optimize on things that you should never have concerned yourself with in the first place. You spend time and effort valiantly improving, enhancing, and adjusting a massive collection of tasks… and half of those tasks are pointless.

This is not productivity. It's distraction.

Getting out of this trap is easier said than done!

Here's how:

Eliminate Anything That Doesn't Need To Be Done

Entrepreneurs or those wanting to work on their personal self-development can often have a hard time identifying what's genuinely their business, and what isn't. Here are some examples of activities and tasks that may genuinely seem relevant... but really aren't:

- You're an artisan who sells bespoke products, but you waste hours every month creating new offerings instead of focusing on a few key products.
- You're in a service industry but waste hours every month on social media branding, fiddling with your website fonts and colors, and changing up your logo.
- You're a businessman wasting hours every month trying to build a coaching course that will realistically bring you zero short- or long-term value.
- You're signed up for several committees and waste hours every month attending meetings and responding to queries that ultimately have nothing to do with you.

You get the idea... the first part of the funnel, eliminate, is about so much more than turning your notifications off. **It's about continually asking yourself which tasks concern you, and which don't.**

Usually, the biggest time sinks and distractions are those activities that put on a pretty convincing disguise, which is why we have to be way more deliberate in applying the funnel than we might at first think.

Be brutally honest and sniff out distractions trying to pass themselves off as work.

Tip: Notice the shape of the funnel? It's an inverted pyramid, and it's that way for a reason. *Only a tiny fraction* of all tasks that come your way ultimately make it through the funnel and into the DO stage.

Moving down the funnel is a process of elimination. You don't begin with the assumption of action, but pass a potential task through a series of filters, only taking action on what remains.

Mindset shift—Be selective, not reactive.

Most of what comes your way should be eliminated, delegated, or automated. Yes, most!

Relevant Chapters to Revisit:

- Chater 2 – The 1-3-5 Rule can help you sort activities and task according to importance
- Chapter 4 – Finding the WHY behind tasks will help you decide whether they ultimately matter
- Chapter 5 – Identify no more than three priorities for your To Do list and set aside the rest
- Chapter 12 – Consider whether there is something you need to be saying "no" to
- Chapter 15 – Use the Touch It Once Principle to get rid of useless zombie tasks

Automate Anything That Doesn't Need a Human Touch

If we're honest, we'll see that not everything that poses as work is work, not everything that claims to be urgent is urgent, and not everything labelled important is important.

But naturally, some things do in fact need to be done. These are the things we consciously allow to fall further down the funnel.

Note: We don't want to waste *any* time and energy on unnecessary tasks, even the time and energy it takes trying to figure out if they can be automated, delegated, etc. That's why the *first* question is always about relevancy, and we make that call decisively and early on.

If a task does have to happen, then the next thing we ask is:

"Is there a way to systematize or automate this?"

Just because it needs to be done, it doesn't mean that a human (specifically you) has to do it.

There is simply no need to trade in your precious, non-renewable time if there is a possibility of handing it over to a tool that will do the same job. Automation does take a little time upfront to organize, but it has a high ROI.

Why don't people automate things more often?

- It's sometimes about ego and control—we think it's more important that *we* do something than that it just gets done
- We're caught in a hustle mindset where we valorize extreme effort, even if nobody requires us to make that effort
- It simply doesn't occur to us that tasks *can* be automated

It can be a very illuminating exercise to sit down with a piece of paper and create two columns:

The first column: All those tasks in your project, business, or enterprise that require your specific human touch, your creativity, your unique attributes and attention.

The second column: All those tasks that can be easily managed by a machine.

The ratio of human to non-human tasks will vary widely, but what matters is that we are not wasting our human time on tasks that could just as easily be done by machines (and yes, any system, tool, or procedure is a kind of machine).

Take a good look at your list. If you are wasting precious time on tasks in the second column, you're not just doing too much, you're actually taking away from all those things in the first column—and remember, there is no machine to do *that*.

Examples:

- Instead of responding manually to various non-essential messages, set up templates or auto-responses
- Instead of wasting time putting together social media posts for your business, and trying to remember when to post them; schedule and automate them, or better yet, hire someone to do it for you
- Instead of personally writing to clients or customers, set up an automated flow of emails, updates, and notifications that you don't have to monitor
- Instead of compiling invoices for orders or tracking those orders manually, use a website with the entire order process automated and synced with your bank

Not all automations are necessarily software apps or products you need to pay for. However, don't automatically assume that it's a bad idea to spend money on something you know you could easily do yourself. The real payoff is in the time you save, and how much *that's* worth. Keep your eye on that when weighing up costs and benefits.

Relevant Chapters to Revisit:

- Chapter 7 – Use the DRY principle, Don't Repeat Yourself, to eliminate repetition
- Chapter 9 – Use an SSOT, Single Source of Truth, to avoid duplicating information
- Chapter 17 – Increase Germane Cognitive load to make your life easier

OK, ready to move one more notch down the funnel?

Delegate Anything That Someone Else Can Do for You

Some tasks can't be eliminated and can't be automated or handed over to a system. They have to be done, and they have to be done by a human. At this point in the funnel, you decide if *you're* that human.

Many people struggle with delegation.

It's not being lazy—it's being selective. You say no to making certain efforts precisely so you can be more effective in making other efforts.

The simple fact is that you can't do everything, nor should you try. You have limited energy and time, and the responsibility of deciding where it gets spent.

There are certain tasks and activities that *only* you can do—focus on those, and vow never to allow other tasks to dilute your efforts there.

Examples:

- Hire an assistant, live or virtual, to take over admin
- Get a professional to create content, do graphic design, film videos, take photos, manage your taxes and accounting, sort out marketing campaigns, and so on
- Ask a colleague or team member more suited to the job to take over

If you're a sole trader, a single service provider, or simply someone trying to improve some aspect of your personal life, there will likely not be much to delegate (or, more realistically, someone to delegate to).

Being frank, delegation may be desirable in some cases but not strictly possible. You simply may not have the money or manpower at your disposal—and that's OK!

If a task finally finds its way to this stage, then it lands squarely on your desk.

This is yours to do.

Luckily, by passing the task through the funnel you can rest assured that it really is relevant, unautomatable, and rightly your responsibility.

The task has been qualified.

The only thing to decide from here is whether to do it now or do it later.

"Is now the right time for this task?"

Isn't it funny how this is often the first question we ask of an incoming task, not the last?

If yes, then focus. Concentrate. Do whatever you can to block off distractions, channel your cognitive resources, and channel your attention to what matters.

If no, then "procrastinate" —although in this case the word means to put things off *in a purposeful way*:

- Schedule a time to revisit the task or take your first action step
- If the task is a little unclear, break it down into chunks, identify the first chunk, then commit some time to tackling it
- You may choose to put the task at the top of the funnel again to process later—it may be clearer what you need to do if you reconsider everything later, with fresh eyes

Relevant Chapters to Revisit:

- Chapter 1 – Cut away mental clutter and be more selective overall
- Chapter 3 – Take proactive control of your time with time blocking
- Chapter 6 and 8 – Create a Slump Mode Protocol that allows you to make the best of down days by focusing on the bare minimum; i.e., No Zero Days
- Chapter 14 – Go into Monk Mode for the most important tasks
- Chapter 16 – Set your own internal milestones and use self-competition to track your progress and keep yourself motivated
- Chapter 19 – Occasionally use the Clean Slate Method to refresh your brain and keep looking at tasks with a renewed perspective.

Conclusion

"The secret to productivity is simplicity."

- **Robin Sharma**

If there are ten rabbits running all over the place, and you hope to catch one, then don't chase all ten. *Just chase one.*

The best routes to "doing more" paradoxically look like "doing less."

In this book we've covered a few productivity approaches that may appear extremely simple on the surface. But that's precisely why they're so powerful.

Whether you call it...

- focus
- discipline
- identifying priorities
- tuning out distractions
- uncovering your Big Why
- or trimming away at waste and excess

...the principle is the same: **Chase less, catch more. Just focus on one rabbit.**

The world is full to bursting with "rabbits", but your goal should never be to become a better rabbit chaser. You don't have to hustle, burn yourself out, or become superhuman. You don't have to sacrifice what matters to you, make time appear out of nowhere, or destroy your mental or physical health to attain what's important to you.

One final rule of thumb we'll close this book with is this: If you feel overwhelmed, confused, vague, lost, frazzled, bored, or otherwise overloaded, then take it as a cue to simplify.

Stop. Take a deep breath. Do one thing that matters, right now. Ignore the rest.

Be decisive, take action, and realize that productivity is a way of life, an attitude, and a habit. One that you cultivate every single day that you choose to wake up and do your best.

Understand that right now, in this very moment of time, you are creating. You are building. You are making tomorrow.

Remember that *you* get to decide what to spend your life on, where your time goes, and what you want to move towards.

Most of all, **keep it simple.**

www.ingramcontent.com/pod-product-compliance
Lightning Source LLC
Chambersburg PA
CBHW060559080526
44585CB00013B/621